W0082039

Martin Sherman was born in Philadelphia. He has lived in London since 1980. His plays include: *Passing By*, *Cracks*, *Rio Grande*, *Bent*, *Messiah*, *When She Danced*, *A Madhouse in Goa*, *Some Sunny Day* and *Rose*. Adaptations include: *Absolutely!* (*Perhaps*) (Pirandello), *The Cherry Orchard* (Chekhov) and *A Passage to India* (from E. M. Forster). Musical: *The Boy from Oz*. His screenplays include: *The Clothes in the Wardrobe* (US title: *The Summer House*), *Alive and Kicking*, *Bent*, *Callas Forever*, *The Roman Spring of Mrs Stone* and *Mrs Henderson Presents*. His plays have been produced in over fifty countries and he has received nominations for two Oliviers, two Tonys and two Baftas.

Martin Sherman

Aristo

based on material from Nemesis *by Peter Evans*

Methuen Drama

Published by Methuen Drama 2008

1 3 5 7 9 10 8 6 4 2

Methuen Drama
A & C Black Publishers Limited
36 Soho Square
London W1D 3QY
www.acblack.com

Based on material from *Nemesis* by Peter Evans

ISBN: 978 1 408 11075 1

A CIP catalogue record for this book
is available from the British Library

Typeset by Country Setting, Kingsdown, Kent
Printed and bound in Great Britain by
CPI Cox & Wyman, Reading, RG1 8EX

This book is produced using paper that is made from wood grown
in managed, sustainable forests. It is natural, renewable and recyclable.
The logging and manufacturing processes conform to the environmental
regulations of the country of origin.

For the Denissi

Mimi
Maria
Sopia
and Maritina

Aristo

Aristo was first presented in the Minerva at Chichester Festival Theatre on 11 September 2008. The cast was as follows:

Aristo	Robert Lindsay
Jackie	Elizabeth McGovern
Costa	Robin Soans
Yanni	John Hodgkinson
Theo	Julius D'Silva
Dimitra	Denise Black
Eleni	June Watson
Maria	Diana Quick
Alexandro	Joe Marsh
Bouzouki Player	Ben Grove

Director Nancy Meckler
Designer Katrina Lindsay
Music and Sound Designer Ilona Sekacz
Lighting Designer Paul Pyant

Characters

Aristo
Jackie
Costa
Yanni
Theo
Dimitra
Eleni
Maria
Alexandro
Bouzouki Player

Act One

Lights rise on the deck of a yacht. **Aristo** *is singing, quietly, to himself, a melancholy melody. He is Greek, in his sixties, dressed in a dinner jacket.*

Aristo (*sings*)
  Tha giriso lipimeni panagia
  Eche gia
  Min kles to marazi
  Mathe filakto na min kremas
  Na les den piraziu
  Tha'rthi aspri emra ke gia mas . . .

Jackie *steps out of the shadows. She is in her thirties. She is American, elegantly dressed.*

Jackie   Please – don't stop.

Aristo   I didn't realise you were there.

Jackie   Didn't you?

Aristo   An interesting question. I may be lying.

Jackie   Oh.

Pause.

Do you often lie?

Aristo   Only when I have to. So, yes, I often lie. But, as you may notice, I always tell the truth about lying.

Jackie   That's refreshing. Most of the people I know really can't tell the difference.

Aristo   Ah. Politicians.

Jackie   I'm afraid so.

Aristo   The god of lies has a soft spot for politics.

Jackie (*laughs*)   Did the Greeks really have a special god for dishonesty?

Aristo   My dear, we had a god for everything. Everything human. It would have been Hermes, as he was also the god of theft. And commerce. They seemed to think the two belong together.

Jackie   Don't they?

Aristo   Of course. In my world, nothing quite adds up as nature intended. Two and two do not necessarily make four, not if four goes against my interests.

Jackie   Do you really admit so easily to being a scoundrel?

Aristo   Yes. Thrilling, isn't it?

Jackie   Well, I don't know . . . (*Laughs.*) Actually, yes.

Aristo   I make deals. The best deals never stand up to moral scrutiny. Every businessman and politician in the world knows that. I'm a pirate. Not unlike your husband.

Jackie   He would never admit to that.

Aristo   Then I *am* unlike him.

Jackie   Possibly. Possibly not.

Pause.

I like pirates. When I was a little girl I was bored to tears with Peter Pan and positively detested Wendy, but I had a huge crush on Captain Hook. I still do, I suppose. He was a bit of a rascal, wasn't he? – dangerous and in danger at the same time – I mean, that ticking clock . . . He had edge. Of course the problem with Captain Hook was his lack of elegance. And he had that really horrid, tatty ship . . .

Aristo   Not a yacht.

Jackie   No. Not a yacht.

Aristo   So your dream man is Captain Hook on a yacht.

Jackie   Umm. Preferably with both hands intact.

Aristo   Ah. As I suspected. You have a carnal soul.

Jackie I am going to tactfully change the subject. Tell me about the song you were singing.

Aristo It concerns an insatiable woman. She must make love ten times a night.

Jackie You don't approve of changing a subject.

Aristo Not unless I do it.

Jackie Then the trick is to make you think you've done it.

Aristo No. I can't be flattered.

Jackie I wouldn't dream of trying.

Aristo Actually the song was about love.

Jackie Love?

Aristo Yes. You know, it's rumoured to be a human emotion. Highly overrated in my opinion. Do you know *rebetiko*?

Jackie I don't think so. Unless it's a wine.

Aristo It's what we call our songs – some of them – the melancholy ones mostly – the ones about misfortunes of fate – the ones played by a bouzouki, which is actually an instrument from antiquity, a favourite of the gods supposedly. These songs are influenced by Turkish melodies, brought here by the Greeks who fled Asia Minor, like my family. Who I will tell you about. This particular song at one point says, 'I have cried salty tears when I am away from you.' *Salty.* It's an old favourite and I am very fond of it although I detest all of its sentiments. After all, the only free people – really free – are those who love nothing or no one. Don't you think?

Jackie I think you're pretending not to be sentimental.

Aristo In other words, I'm lying. Well, it's as I said. Second nature. Although I am not sentimental. I must warn you about that. Do not imbue me with American qualities. I'm from a much older race. You go back to the *Mayflower*; we go back to Mount Olympus.

Jackie Well then, you were not lying.

Aristo   Don't be silly. Of course I was. Do you see those lights on the shore?

Jackie   I believe *you* have just changed the subject.

Aristo   I have. Look at the lights, please. It's Izmir. Where I was born. It was called Smyrna then.

Jackie   Wasn't Homer born there?

Aristo   He was. As well.

Jackie   Then Smyrna was twice blessed.

Aristo   Precisely. I'll show it to you tomorrow. I'll show you my father's warehouse, if you like; it's still there. He was a tobacco merchant. Did well for a Greek living in Asia Minor. I'll show you where Fahria's was. The local whorehouse. Do I shock you?

Jackie   I think you're trying to. Actually, my father was known to visit whorehouses. I find that not unacceptable.

Aristo   I was very popular at Madame Fahria's when I was a teenager. Because I carried vast supplies of my father's finest tobaccos with me.

Jackie   Is that where you learned about commerce?

Aristo   Of course. And even there I got the better deal. Fahria's would have suited you.

Jackie   Careful.

Aristo   That was a compliment. I'll show you the port tomorrow, which is where I first saw the Fourth Turkish Cavalry the night they rode into Izmir, then Smyrna, intent on driving out the Greek population. They were dressed completely in black and carried their scimitars unsheathed and drawn. Have you ever seen a scimitar? It would be unusual if you had; in Washington the weapons are mostly unseen, isn't that true? No matter, I'll show you one; I have a scimitar locked away on the boat. I have no idea why. I should hang it in a stateroom, but it might seem vulgar. I realise perfectly that you might consider other sections of this yacht vulgar, in concert with most of the fashionable people who snicker at this uppity Greek behind his back. They focus on my bar stools – the ones made of whales' scrotums. But if I had simply pretended it was some kind of leather they would have admired them. Why pretend? Don't you agree?

Jackie   That was a breathtaking subject change.

Aristo   Not necessarily. The subject remains carnal. I'm about to tell you how I was fucked by a Turkish soldier.

Jackie (*laughs*)   Bravo. I didn't see that coming. Were you really? Tell me. In detail. Please.

Aristo   Oh, I intend to. I was sixteen, it was 1919, and the Turks arrested my father and sent him to prison. Our house was commandeered by a young lieutenant who was rather extraordinary, possessing both taste and curiosity, qualities wasted killing people. I liked him. He took to me. We became lovers. Which allowed me to sneak food and money to my father in prison, but I cannot – or will not – pretend my capitulation was based solely on that. I enjoyed it. You see, he inserted his cock into rather surprising and delicate parts of my body, and I could feel its rhythm, its music, its sometimes senseless lurching, at other times its sublime control, and pleasure and pain were indistinguishable from one another – are you enjoying this, by the way?

Jackie   Well, it's not Homer.

Aristo   Good. Then you are. The point, my dear, is – whilst being fucked, I had a revelation. This, I thought, must be, to some degree at least, what a woman feels with a man inside of her. I had discovered a great secret, a secret that would make me an extraordinary lover. I knew from that moment on the sensations a woman has when she is being made love to. And so it only follows that I know how to prolong that pleasure. When I screw a woman, I am in it for the long haul, so to speak. I inhabit the house. Some men just drop in for a visit. Isn't that true? That question is purely rhetorical.

Jackie   Perhaps that entire story is as well. Perhaps it's the biggest lie of all.

Aristo   Perhaps. Do consult your sister. I will confess a very recent lie to you. The one you suspected. I knew you were there, listening. I know every footstep on my boat, feel every shadow. I never have to turn around to know what's behind me. Or ahead of me, for that matter. The past, the future, all connect when I'm here. Here on my ship. Captain Hook with all my hands on deck.

Jackie (*stares at him for a second, then – softly*)   Tick-tock . . . tick-tock . . .

Aristo   As crocodiles go, you're very attractive. So tell me, what do you make of Hook's new surroundings?

Jackie   I feel like Alexander entering the tent of Darius.

Aristo   Oh?

Jackie   'So this it seems is what it is to be a king.'

Silence.

Aristo   I see. Except Alexander had just defeated Darius.

Jackie   He had indeed.

Aristo (*smiles*)   Never anticipate. Tomorrow I'll show you the street I grew up on, the house I lived in. I'll show you the bed in the house on the street where Aristotle Socrates Onassis grew into a man. I was, as you know, named for not one, but two philosophers. Tomorrow I'll show you whatever you need to see so you can understand me. And desire me. I'll show you an old life, and I promise you, my dear Mrs Kennedy – or may I now, after this illuminating conversation, address you as Jacqueline? – or perhaps even Jackie? – a new life as well. I am delighted you accepted my invitation to join us on this cruise. I shall see you in the morning.

The lights fade, as the stage is consumed by music.

Lights rise on three **Musicians** *sitting onstage. Two play bouzoukis, the other a violin. They are playing the song* **Aristo** *was singing.*

*Three men (**Costa**, **Yanni** and **Theo**) and two women (**Dimitra** and **Eleni**) mingle among the **Musicians**. Some are singing. Some stop, and the others pick up the song. They are all over sixty and tastefully dressed.*

*They are the **Chorus**.*

Chorus
> *Tha potiso m'ena dakri mou almiro*
> *Ton kero*
> *Pikra kalokeria ematha konta sou na perno*
> *Nekra peristeria*
> *Gemise I avgi ton ourano . . .*

Yanni *opens a bottle of wine and pours glasses for the others.* **Eleni** *is passing around pastries.*

Eleni   I baked these . . .

Costa (*referring to the music*)   This was his favourite song . . .

Dimitra   We know, we know . . .

Eleni (*handing pastry to* **Theo**)   Here, it's good for you, you don't eat enough . . .

Theo (*laughs*)   You're treating me like a grandson . . .

Eleni   I wish I had a grandson . . .

They all sit in chairs and, together, they conclude the song.

Chorus
> *Tha giriso lipimeni panagia*
> *Eche gia*
> *Min kles to marazi*
> *Mathe filako na min kremas*
> *Na les den pirazi*
> *That'rthi aspri mera ke gia mas.*

Costa *rises and addresses the audience.*

Costa   What can I possibly tell you? In antiquity there were gods. They shared all of mankind's virtues and faults and embodied all human concepts and emotions. But the gods went to extremes; although they were like humans in many ways, they behaved as humans did not dare. And, of course, they possessed magical – supernatural – powers. The gods were notorious humanphiles, however; they had an unnatural attraction to the cream of man and womankind, whom they were prone to ravage. And so demigods were born and, later still, those who the mythologists called heroes, who were not necessarily heroic, not in our terms, but behaved with the sweep and grandeur of the gods and yet remained humanly vulnerable. Movie stars and politicians come to mind. And, let's face it, it is difficult not to walk in their shadows. I, for one, certainly do. I am the second in command to Aristotle Onassis. Aristo. Ari. I share his secrets and execute his commands. I touch the sun, so to speak, and of course I sustain burns, but, really, I'd rather do so than walk placidly on earth, day after boring day. I suppose I become more than I am, and yet also somewhat less than me. My name is Costa. All right. My job is to explain things to you so you will know exactly what we are dealing with. How on earth . . . Well, with a little bit of help.

Yanni *brings on a blackboard and chalk, and places them next to* **Costa***, who acknowledges the blackboard.*

Costa   This should make things easier – eventually, at least.

Dimitra   Oh dear, the blackboard.

Eleni   Shh . . .

Hands her another piece of pastry.

Costa   Now, you have just witnessed Aristotle Onassis –

Writes 'Aristotle Onassis' on the blackboard.

– that's two 's's in the centre – one of the world's richest men, a notorious shipowner and much else – and my boss – my, in the classical sense, hero – in an early encounter with Jacqueline Kennedy –

Writes 'Jacqueline Kennedy' on the blackboard.

– wife of the 35th President of the United States. Her baby, Patrick, had died three days after his premature birth in Boston. Lee Radziwell, Jackie's sister and Aristo's current mistress –

Writes 'Lee Radziwell' on the blackboard, and draws lines connecting her to Onassis and Jacqueline Kennedy.

– had urged Aristo to invite her depressed sister onto his yacht for a restorative cruise. It is 1963, by the way. Jacqueline accepted the invitation, despite the chequered history of Onassis and the Kennedy clan. There had long been bad blood between Aristo and her brother-in-law. That's Robert Kennedy. Brother to the 35th President of the United States. Attorney-General and heir apparent. Bobby.

Writes 'Robert Kennedy' on blackboard and draws lines connecting him to Jacqueline and Onassis.

From now on, whenever a new name is mentioned, he will draw it on the blackboard, and connect it by lines, if necessary, to other names. Names already mentioned might reappear, with new connective lines to be made.

Now – Bobby Kennedy and Aristotle Onassis met for the first time at a cocktail party given by the English socialite Pamela Churchill at the Plaza Hotel in New York City. They took an instant, visceral dislike to one another. This was in the spring of 1953, the year Jacqueline Lee Bouvier married John F. Kennedy. Pamela Churchill was a shrewd networker long before the term had been invented. She was the former wife of Randolph Churchill, the drunken son of the former British Prime Minister, Winston Churchill, who was himself a frequent guest on the yacht of Aristotle Onassis. She had known Bobby since 1938 when his father, Joseph P. Kennedy, was the American Ambassador to England. She was a friend of Bobby's sister, Kathleen Kennedy, and indeed at the age of eighteen, whilst a weekend guest at the Kennedy home, had been raped by Kathleen's father when he slipped into her bed late one night. That's the aforementioned Joseph P., who, years before, had been the lover of the movie star Gloria Swanson, who had later and coincidentally had an affair with Aristotle Onassis, who in the early 1940s was just beginning to climb from the ruins of Smyrna to the world of maritime tycoons, and was sleeping with other movie stars as well, such as Veronica Lake and Paulette Goddard, who later married the German novelist Erich Maria Remarque, who had been a lover of Marlene

Dietrich, who had, on separate occasions, slept with both John F. Kennedy, and his father Joseph P., the raping ambassador. Aristo also had an affair with the French actress Simone Simon, who gave him a venereal disease, which he was able to quickly cure, unlike John F. Kennedy, who carried symptoms of *his* venereal disease with him for the rest of his life, infecting Jackie, who would possibly later infect Ari. Aristotle's infatuation with movie stars ended when he paid court to Tina Livanos, the younger daughter of the greatest Greek shipowning family, who he eventually married. Tina's older sister Eugenia would marry Aristo's chief business rival, Stavros Niarchos, who was, incidentally, a former lover of Pamela Churchill's, as indeed was Ari. I would call Niarchos Onassis' nemesis, but that word is better applied to Bobby Kennedy. Like Onassis he had a penchant for movie stars, although not to the degree of his brother John F., the 35th President of the United States, and indeed they both had famously bedded Marilyn Monroe, who, you will be relieved to know, never met Aristo. Although he did offer her his yacht after she was fired by her movie studio, Twentieth Century Fox, which was run by Spyros Skouros, a fellow Greek, who happened to own a fleet of container ships, which Onassis had invested ten million dollars in; ships that would cut union costs by 60 per cent, thus earning the enmity of the labour racketeer Jimmy Hoffa, who was an associate of the Mafia boss, Sam Giancana, whose mistress was Judith Campbell, who was also sleeping with John F. Kennedy, whose brother Robert was an implacable enemy of Jimmy Hoffa, and had written a book about their conflict, the film rights of which were held by Spyros Skouros, who was, needless to say, a former lover of Marilyn Monroe.

Pause.

I'm exhausted. If you find this a little heady, I can assure you – it is. But the secrets of powerful men, the men who rule the world, who are the real, if sometimes covert, centres of power, read astonishingly like a cheap gossip column. Well, actually not. Gossip columns are comparatively tame. Real life is far more complicated. Where were we?

Yanni *walks up to him.*

Yanni   We're up to Jiddah.

Costa   Oh yes. May I introduce Yanni –

Yanni   Yes, please. Financial adviser to Aristotle Onassis. Perhaps it would be easier if I explained this part.

Costa   Only if you get straight to the point.

Yanni (*pushing the blackboard aside*)   Of course. Now, question mark. Why did Aristotle Onassis hate Robert Kennedy? Now, seriously speaking, I would say, if you allow me – Aristotle Onassis hated Robert Kennedy because of the Jiddah Agreement. Period. Full stop. That's my opinion.

Costa   Just give the basic –

Yanni   Yes. Yes. If I may. Aristotle Onassis was working on, if I may be allowed to say so, an extraordinary deal with the Saudi Arabians that would have given him the rights to ship the bulk of the oil flowing out of the Arabian kingdom. Now, bear in mind, this would mean Aristotle Onassis would have had a monopoly on the transport of more than forty-five million tons of Saudi oil a year. I have to confess this would have made him as powerful as any nation state. Exclamation point! It would have undermined a previous treaty signed by four major American companies – their names, may I tell you, are Standard Oil, Mobil, Exxon and Texaco – and again, bear in mind, this would in effect break the chain of mutual dependency between the American oil barons and the Arabian princelings. Or put it, if I may, in another way, it meant that Saudi Arabia and Aristole Onassis would, between them, control the means of oil production and distribution, thus empowering the Arab nation to do without America. This deal, I would like to say, was signed by the Saudi foreign minister and waited only royal approval . . . dot, dot, dot . . .

Costa (*wheeling the blackboard on again and supplanting* **Yanni**) Fine. Thank you.

Theo (*motioning for* **Yanni** *to sit again*)   Yanni.

Yanni *sits.*

Costa (*writing connective lines on the blackboard again*)   Now − let
us recap. The Livanos sisters − Tina and Eugenia, remember?
Tina married to Onassis, Eugenia married to Niarchos. Tina,
needless to say, was sleeping with her sister's husband. She
informed him about Aristo's impending − and top secret − deal
with the Saudis. Niarchos was Onassis' most implacable rival.
He was determined to stop the deal and knew that only the
Americans could do so. Niarchos was, among many other
things, a valued CIA informant, and he passed the information
on to them. The Saudis finally backed down under pressure
from the American government and the Jiddah Agreement
was cancelled. The CIA was eager to hide Niarchos'
involvement − they protected their informants − so they created
a smokescreen that would make it appear that Robert Kennedy
was responsible. They were aware that Onassis already disliked
Kennedy because the young lawyer, working for a Senate
committee, had recently made headlines attacking Greek
shipowners for trading with Red China. Clues were planted
that implied it was Bobby who had destroyed the Jiddah
Agreement and Onassis bought it. Dulles had, as it happens, a
score to settle with Kennedy, as Bobby had recently worked as a
lawyer for Joseph McCarthy's infamous Senate subcommittee.
McCarthy had levelled particularly vicious attacks on the State
Department, which was run by John Foster Dulles, the brother
of Allan Dulles; and thus setting up McCarthy's acolyte,
Robert Kennedy, was a source of enormous satisfaction to
the Dulles brothers. Aristo was, of course, devastated by the
destruction of the deal, but several months later he received a
tip from Pamela's ex-husband Randolph who had heard from
his father Winston that the British Prime Minister, Anthony
Eden, was planning to attack the Suez Canal, along with the
French and Israelis. This meant that oil supplies to Europe
and the United States would be forced to go around the Cape
of Good Hope, a journey twice as long as through Suez and
additional tankers would be needed. Onassis held his ships
back, preventing them from accepting other charters, and
when the invasion occurred was the only shipowner with most

of his fleet available. The American oil companies begged him for the use of his boats, and so the same corporations that had set out to destroy him made him into one of the richest men in the world. There's nothing like a success story, is there? Now what have I left out? Oh, well, did I mention the other reason the CIA wanted to protect Niarchos? The CIA was run by Allan Dulles, who, as it happens, was sleeping with Queen Fredericka of Greece, a liaison brokered by Niarchos himself. Dulles had to make certain that his affair with Fredericka remained a secret; he certainly didn't want Onassis snooping around. Fredericka, by the way, was a cousin of the Duke of Kent, who was rumoured to be the real father of the publisher Michael Canfield, who was the first husband of Lee Bouvier, sister to Jacqueline, who was married to the 35th President of the United States. Lee's second husband was an impoverished Polish prince, Stanislas Radziwell, who financially existed on money stolen from the Polish Red Cross and was actually in love with the heiress Charlotte Ford, who later briefly married Stavros Niarchos. Radziwell looked on benignly as his wife began her affair with Aristotle Onassis and then brought her sister Jacqueline onto his yacht and into the hands of Fate.

Maria Callas *strides on. She looks at* **Costa** *with contempt.*

Maria   There is someone you forgot.

Maria *scrawls the word 'Callas' across the entire blackboard, obliterating the other names.*

Maria   The rest are pygmies!

She walks away, furious.

Dimitra *goes to* **Costa**.

Dimitra   Aren't you ashamed, you foolish little man? You talk of gods! Pah, pah, pah! There are no gods any more, but there was a goddess. And he destroyed her. What kind of hero is our dear Mr Onassis then? What kind of hero?

Maria *addresses* **Dimitra**.

Maria   Dimitra . . .

Dimitra   Yes, Madame Callas?

Maria   Were there unmade beds?

Dimitra   No, Madame Callas.

Maria   No one else slept in his room?

Dimitra   No, Madame Callas.

Maria   Are you certain?

Dimitra   The ship's housekeeper knows everything, Madame Callas.

Maria   Yes, of course . . . Forgive me.

Pause.

He slept alone?

Dimitra   Yes, Madame Callas.

Maria *goes into her apartment.*

Dimitra (*to audience*)   I lied. I had to. How could I tell her?

Costa   Yes, she lied. Aristotle Onassis and Jacqueline Kennedy consummated their flirtation on the Ionian Sea, where the bright currents of the Aegean flow into Homer's 'wine-dark' waters. It was not only Jacqueline's sister who was displaced in his affections but also his real leading lady, the world's most revered opera star, Maria Callas. (*To* **Dimitra**.) Forgive me, Dimitra. I left her out because I wanted her to have some peace. (*To audience.*) Her relationship with Aristo was the primary cause of his divorce from Tina. Madame Callas wasn't like the rest of Aristo's women. They had both known the severities of war, they had both overcome great difficulties to achieve riches and extraordinary fame. They fell in love with each other's past.

A recording of Puccini's 'O mio babbino caro' is heard. **Maria** *sits in her apartment, listening to it.*

Dimitra   And then he destroyed her.

Costa   Yes, I have to concede, he destroyed her.

Maria (*looking at them*)   That's nonsense.

Dimitra   He destroyed your voice.

Eleni *and* **Theo**   He destroyed her voice.

Maria   Stop it! Don't say that. You must not hate him for something he did not do. I destroyed my voice.

Chorus   No, no . . .

Dimitra   Listen to your voice . . .

Maria   I do. Every night. I listen to it. Every night. But when I am with him, on his island, on the boat, there is no need. Don't you understand? I feel the wind across my face. I look at the sea, look at the sky. How can I feel special when I stare at infinity? What's a *voice*? It's not a sound nature intended. Does someone shouting 'bravo' substitute for the sea? How dare they give us the name 'star' when the real thing sits in an unknowable universe? My nights on his ship taught me humility.

Pause.

Everything I'm saying is rubbish. He wanted me as a woman. No one ever had before. It's as simple as that. No, it's not simple. He's a brute. Maybe I need that. No, that's not true. I wanted to stop. Year after year of rehearsing, arguing, primping, remembering – do you realise what an opera singer has to *memorise*? The scores in foreign languages, the intricate notes, and in every city, a different staging for the same piece – so in Milan you move to the right for 'O mio babbino caro', in Rome you stand still, in Paris you sit, in London you fall to your knees. Suppose, God forbid, you fall to your knees in Rome? Our brains are too stuffed with notes and foreign words and conflicting moves – there is no space left to take in the sea or the night sky or a man's embrace. No, that's not it. I can't explain it. What I do know is, it is not difficult being swept off one's feet. Living with the consequences is the hard part. So for years I did not sing, or sang intermittently, which is fatal. And now my voice is gone. Gone. I destroyed it, not Aristo.

Dimitra   Poor woman.

Eleni   She is too modest.

Theo   She doesn't know.

Yanni   She won't admit to it.

Dimitra   Forgive me, Madame Callas, but it's inescapable, he ruined you.

Maria   Ruined! What a word!

Pause.

You must be kinder.

Costa   I love him, Madame Callas, but he is about to throw you over for the one woman in the world more famous than you.

Maria   Who, may I remind you, is married. To the most powerful man in the world. No, not even Aristo can compare with that. He will do no such thing.

Her voice on the recording reaches a crescendo.

Listen. Did you hear that? What I was? Yes, I sit every night in my apartment when I am not with him and I listen to what God gave me, and what I – *I* – threw away. Now all I am is his. Nothing else. His. Of course he will sleep with other women, he's a Greek man, so what? I am a Greek woman – I know he will come back to me. I am his. Listen. It's not just the high notes. It's more. Listen.

Gunshots.

The music and **Maria**'s *apartment fade.*

Gunshots again.

Dimitra   Listen.

Yanni   Dare I say the most famous gunshots in the world? I'm serious.

Costa (*to audience*)   How many? Well – that will always be in dispute. So. John F. Kennedy, the 35th President of the United States, is assassinated by . . . no, *that* you know. But what you probably don't know – what even I, Aristo's closest confidant, still find – well, astonishing – is that Onassis flew to Washington the next day and stayed at the White House – was a guest at *the White House* – until the funeral. Invited by Lee Radziwell, presumably at the request of her sister Jacqueline. He was there the night before the funeral . . . in the same room as Robert Kennedy.

Aristo *is sitting at his desk.. He opens a bottle of wine.* **Costa** *enters the room.* **Aristo** *looks up.*

Aristo   Have a glass.

Pours two glasses of wine.

Costa   Thank you.

Aristo   From our vineyards.

Costa   Yes, I can see.

Pause.

So?

Aristo   So?

Costa   What happened?

Aristo   You *know* what happened. It was on television, it's in every paper, you've seen it all. (*Brushes newspapers on his desk aside.*) Not a single newspaper says I was there. Funny how they always miss the big story. Actually, there was no story. I paid my respects. That's all. (*Drinks.*) Excellent wine. I was sober the entire time. That was quite an accomplishment. Stillness. Sometimes you achieve victory through stillness. But it isn't easy. (*Looks at the bottle.*) What year is it? (*Laughs.*) I hate people who ask that.

Costa   Aristo, tell me what happened.

Aristo   Nothing happened. You're such an old gossip. Nothing happened. It was a funeral. *But* you would have been proud of me. I didn't drink. And I didn't let them get me.

Costa   Get you?

Aristo   Indeed. Oh, now you're curious. Aren't you? (*Pours himself another drink.*) I suppose I should smell the aroma? (*Smiles.*) No. I will trust.

Pause.

His brother. His brother. Well, well. They were all drunk. In the family dining room the night before the funeral. Bobby and his friends. They were singing Irish songs. It was what they call a wake, which is a very strange name, since it implies consciousness. The women were upstairs. Bobby apologised to me. For the noise. He didn't want to offend my European sensibilities. I explained that we also sing when we are sad. I even gave him a bit of a song.

Sings.

> *Ilie fonia pos afises na gini to kako*
> *Skotosane to stavraeto*
> *Ke ton avgerino*
> *Kato sto stavrodromi*
> *Skotosane to nio.*

Pause.

I told him it was about a man who has fallen before his time. 'They killed the golden eagle, The morning star . . . ' He made a face, said it was too pretty. Not his taste. 'Neither are you, Mr Onassis. For Christ's sake, *my brother is dead!*' he shouted. 'What are you doing in our house?' (*Pours another glass for* **Costa**.) Have another.

Costa   *And* . . .

Aristo   And? And nothing. I was very calm. But he was beside himself. He said that he had been attempting through purely legal means, of course, to keep me from ever entering the United States again. And now I was there in the United States, in the White House, at his brother's funeral. Now, my friend, you must understand, he does not revere irony. He dislikes it; it's a Greek export. He kept offering me drinks and I kept refusing. I was determined to stay sober. I knew that would annoy him. I said the White House suggested dignity and I wouldn't presume to get drunk there. 'You won't let me get under your skin?' he said. 'No, no,' I said. 'I won't.' And I didn't. I didn't. So. That's what happened. Nothing.

Costa   I don't believe you. You're much too satisfied with yourself.

Aristo   Well, why not? I returned with a present.

Takes a linen napkin out of his pocket.

Bobby. It's a teenage name, isn't it? Someone with bad skin who takes you to the high-school dance. Bobby. Well, he began to tell the others about my money. He said I owned Monaco, which isn't strictly true. He said I owned my own airline, which is true. He said I owned much too much. Suggested I give it away. And then he grabs this napkin from the table and takes out a pen and proceeds to write on it. He was amusing his drunken Irish friends the night before they buried his brother. 'Aristotle Onassis,' he writes. 'Aristotle Socrates Onassis,' I said. Well, 'I, Aristotle Socrates Onassis, hereby give fifty per cent of my fortune to . . . ' and then he was stuck for a minute . . . so he has a little mini-Kennedy conference with himself, trying to decide where to take this joke, and then he has an inspiration! 'I, Aristotle Socrates Onassis, hereby give fifty per cent of my fortune to the poor of . . . Latin America . . . ' (*Pours himself another drink.*) They were drinking hard whiskey, of course. Not wine. And do you know why he chose Latin America? It turns out that fucker knows everything about me. How I got my start in Buenos Aires, for example. 'Some cigarette scheme,' he said, 'introducing Turkish tobacco to Argentina. Made your first bundle.' Oh yes, he expressed things very eloquently. Bundle! Well, there's truth in the word. I could see him studying my face – he wanted to see if I was shocked that he knew so much. And then – and he said this would impress me – he also knew that I was fucking an opera singer then – an earlier opera singer – and he pretended to fish for her name. 'Muzio, was that it, Claudine?' No, 'Claudia,' I said. Claudia. 'Well, close enough,' he said. Yes. Close enough. I *was* impressed.

He polishes off the wine and hands the empty bottle to **Yanni***.*

Aristo   Our island grapes are unappreciated. Of course, every Greek island makes its own wine. Ours is better, don't you think?

Costa *hands him another bottle.*

Costa   And the point . . .

Aristo   Ah! The point! The point was, the FBI had files that detailed every moment of my life, every deal I'd ever made, every woman I'd ever fucked – and Bobby boy had read them! On the beach, I imagine, like some summer novel, cheap but unputdownable. And then, of course, he couldn't resist a sanctimonious little lecture. 'You know, I wouldn't care, finally, finally, I wouldn't care,' he said, 'if somewhere in those voluminous files there was one kind deed, one act of humanity, some gesture to someone less fortunate than yourself. Grabbing is all right – we all grab – but you have to give as well, that's the essence of a workable society, isn't it? – grab *and* give? It's the basis of democracy, which, yes, don't tell me, is a Greek word. I've memorised your files. Claudia Muzio, see? *Memorised!* I know exactly who you are.' 'Then you are more fortunate than I,' I said. (*Looks at the napkin.*) 'I, Aristotle Socrates Onassis, hereby give fifty per cent of my considerable fortune' – I added considerable – 'to the poor of Latin America.' 'In perpetuity' – I added that as well; might as well give it some style. I dated it and signed it, and he held it up, but no one laughed. The joke had lost its . . . fizz. Perhaps they remembered why they were there. He just stared at me. 'I can't get your goat,' he said. 'No,' I said, quietly – *calmly* – 'you can't.' 'My brother is dead,' he said. 'You may not realise it – or care – but the future of this country is dead as well. *Why are you here?*'

Pause.

Well, I didn't answer, did I?

Pause.

And that was my night at the White House.

Pause.

Stillness, you see. It works.

Rises – and, with great difficulty, tears the linen napkin into small strips and throws them aside.

The skinny, shit-faced, puke-smelling, ass-eating little runt! Get my goat! Goat is a Greek delicacy. We eat them *and* fuck them!

Walks over to the **Chorus**.

And I'll fuck him and eat him too and spit him out and little pieces of him will scatter over the earth and land on outdoor barbecues in Minnesota and Dubrovnik and Thesonniki and be consumed as little specs of ash on second-rate, under-cooked souvlaki! Get my goat! My 'goat' has just begun!

He grabs another bottle of wine and drinks it down almost in one gulp. He grabs a piece of pastry and devours it.

Aristo   What's this?

Eleni   Just a pastry.

Aristo   But with a syrup . . .

Eleni   Rose-flavoured . . .

Aristo   Yes, I know. My grandmother used to make them every Sunday. In Smyrna. You can smash the vase, but the scent of the flowers never quite goes away. Isn't that true?

He snaps his fingers to the **Musicians**, *who begin a song.*

Aristo (*sings*)
   Imaste alania
   Thialehta pethia mesa stin piatsa
   Ke then tin tromazoun
   I fourtounes tin thika mas ratsa . . .

The **Chorus** *joins* **Aristo**.

Chorus *and* **Aristo**
   Ti ta thes, Ti ta thes
   Panda etsi in e zoi
   Tha yelas ke tha kles
   Vrathi ke proi . . .

Aristo *starts to dance. The others applaud in time and some start to dance with him. Finally, the song finishes.* **Yanni** *hands* **Aristo** *another bottle of wine.*

Aristo *drinks, then goes to* **Theo**.

Aristo   My son? Tell me the truth. How is he doing?

Theo   Wonderfully, Mr Onassis.

Aristo   The truth. Don't butter me up.

Theo   Alexandro has turned the travel bureau into a profitable operation. Surely you know that.

Aristo   Of course I know that. I just wanted to hear you say it. It gives me . . . fatherly pride. Pleasure. He's a good boy, isn't he?

Theo   He is, Mr Onassis. Everyone at the office loves him.

Pause.

Aristo (*quietly*)   Everyone loves him?

Theo   You can be very proud of him. He's considerate, courteous . . . he's an extraordinarily nice young man.

Aristo   *Nice!* There has never been a *nice* Onassis! Where is the bastard? I'll tear him limb from limb. Not to mention considerate and courteous! Hasn't he learned anything from me?

Theo (*amused*)   Well, actually . . .

Aristo   It's not a joke. You have no idea how *dangerous* it is to be nice in my world. I am afraid for him. Do you understand? It's that woman, isn't it? That bitch. She's pasteurised him. She's made him safe to drink. I'll break her legs. I'll scar her face. I promise you! I will not have a nice son!

Aristo *storms off.*

Theo (*to audience*)   When you work for Mr Onassis you invariably say the wrong thing. But he gets over it. The storm arrives from nowhere. But then it leaves. And you're still standing.

Costa (*to audience, with the blackboard, now wiped clean*)   Now. Here we go. His two children by Tina –

Writes their names.

Alexandro and Christina. Alexandro is . . . nice, and Christina difficult. Alexandro was put to work at a subsidiary of Olympic Airways and, as Theo has said, did very well. He is in love with the former Fiona Campbell-Walter, subsequently the former Baroness Thyssen-Bournemisea, sixteen years his senior. As for Olympic Airways, it is owned by Ari. The Greek government sold it to him for a mere two million dollars and he transformed it overnight into a world-class airline. He is the only private citizen alive who owns a national airline. He worries about his children and he detests Fiona Campbell-Walter Thyssen-Bournemesia, perhaps because she's independent, or perhaps, it has been suggested, because she prefers not the father, but the son.

Aristo's *house.* **Aristo** *and* **Alexandro**.

Aristo   Your mother says she's a call girl. That this Fiona of yours was paid a hundred thousand dollars to spend one night with King Farouk in St Moritz.

Alexandro   But he's obese. That's too low a price.

Aristo   Then she's a stupid call girl.

Alexandro   Not even you believe this one, Papa.

Aristo   Don't use that fucking word. It's so sentimental. I'm bored with you. Go away. Do you ever hit her?

Alexandro   Of course not.

Aristo   Are you faithful?

Alexandro   Yes.

Aristo   I despair, I despair. Where's the *passion*? If you fight, if you strike her, if you walk away, it means there is some kind of feeling, and feeling is what's important, feeling means you are alive, unlike politeness, which is antiseptic, which is a desert, and then, of course, you *come back*, and you cry, and

you say, 'I am sorry, my love,' and you buy her a diamond.
Then you are a man.

Alexandro   I'm leaving.

Aristo   Not until I say you can go.

Alexandro   You told me to go away.

Aristo   I didn't mean it.

Alexandro   What *do* you mean?

Aristo   Very little. Get out. She's a spy.

Alexandro (*starts to leave*)   Goodnight.

Aristo (*throws a glass at him*)   Don't you dare walk out on me.
Your mother told me that Niarchos is paying her to spy on us.

Alexandro   She's sleeping with Niarchos.

Aristo   Fiona?

Alexandro   Mother.

Aristo   That's beside the point. Your girl is a spy.

Alexandro   She doesn't need to be. Uncle Stavro has bugged
all our houses. And you've bugged all of his. Actually, you've
bugged all of *our* houses as well. Silly for you to ask me
questions when you've already heard the answers on tape.

Aristo   Look at you, standing there, looking bewildered, as
always . . .

Grabs **Alexandro** *and hugs him.*

Aristo   You're a goddamned baby. Useless.

Pause.

You're a good boy. (*Kisses him.*) Your mother wouldn't lie.

Alexandro   She always lies. Just like you. Did you actually
ever love her?

Aristo   There were moments. Life has moments. And there's a kind of satisfaction. And then the moment passes. And you want more. It will pass for you too. One day you wake up and look at her sleeping next to you and have nothing but contempt.

Alexandro   For her or yourself?

Aristo   Does it matter? It's still contempt.

Alexandro   What happened to the passion you were talking about?

Aristo   You still have the passion. But for someone else. How did you come out of my belly so green? If this Fiona is a spy I'll find out. And then if you don't get rid of her, I will for you.

Alexandro, *shocked, pulls away and leaves. He walks among the* **Chorus**.

Dimitra   Don't take him so seriously.

Theo   He doesn't mean it.

Alexandro   He does. He never makes empty threats.

Costa   He's jealous because she's never given him a second look.

Yanni   In my opinion, he wants her himself.

Costa   That's what I just said.

Yanni   Oh.

Alexandro *begins to strip off his clothes.* **Eleni** *goes to him.*

Eleni   Alexandro, what are you doing?

Alexandro   Going for a swim.

Eleni   In the middle of the night? You'll catch cold.

Alexandro   You're not my nanny any more.

Eleni   Oh, I am. Nannies are for life. I still look after you, but at a distance. And you're just the same. You always got upset when you saw him. You still do.

Alexandro   He could harm her.

Eleni   He won't.

Alexandro   But he *could*. Don't put it past him.

Eleni   She loves you. That's all that should matter to you.

Alexandro   That's all that does matter to me. Which is why I'm afraid for her. You know, the first time I ever saw her she was climbing out of a sports car in a snowstorm and I thought she was on fire. But it was just her hair, her incredible red hair, falling on her shoulders, like Rome burning. She was the most exciting woman I had ever seen.

Eleni   How old were you then?

Alexandro   Twelve. But I knew what I was doing when I was –

Eleni (*laughs*)   Twelve.

Alexandro   Yes. And I suppose being attracted to flames was not surprising with my lineage. I was determined I would marry her when I grew up. And six years later I asked my mother to invite her to a dinner party, and then . . . well, we've not been apart since. Fiona's only three years younger than my mother, so my mother hates her almost as much as my father does, but she's not as dangerous as he is. What's so strange is that she's the only woman I ever really wanted and the only woman I do want and the only woman I ever shall want, which of course makes me some sort of a freak, doesn't it, in my father's eyes at least, and in the eyes of his friends and his business associates, and in fact all of society. 'That man will only ever love one woman!' They should put me in a cage in a carnival. It's too confusing. I have to swim. (*He is now naked.*) What are you looking at? You've seen me naked so many times.

Eleni   But now you're grown up. You're like a young god.

Alexandro   A lot of good it will do me.

Eleni   Why are you swimming in the middle of the night?

Alexandro   So I can think out loud. It's the one place he can't bug. There are no microphones in the sea.

He walks away, into the sea.

Eleni (*prays*)   Poseidon! Do you hear me? Yes, I still believe in you. You're so simple. You're just the sea. Just the huge, unfathomable, unknowable sea. Be gentle with my Alexandro. Don't send one of your sudden midnight storms, don't whip up your waves, don't play games with the tides. Let him swim in calm waters. I worry about him. I am afraid for him.

Costa (*prays*)   My dear Athena, goddess of wisdom, try to give me a drop, just a drop of that precious commodity. Am I being too modest? Perhaps. I was born in your image. I do possess some wisdom. But I am no longer certain what Aristo is thinking. He's been in the habit of telling me everything – no matter how venal – but suddenly I sense secrets. He is keeping something from me. Perhaps he resents what I have to offer – common sense. Tell me, why is wisdom so uncomfortable, why are the wise so unhappy, and why do people tire of us so easily? You never had a childhood, Athena, did you? Your legend says you were born fully grown. So we were never children, is that it? We are damned to being grown-up in perpetuity. What's so smart about that?

Yanni (*prays*)   Question mark. Why does Mr Onassis want to make financial deals with villains, like the Russians, and the colonels, those little, can I be precise, fascists who have seized control of Greece? Do you know what I'm saying, Hermes? Bear in mind, business only really works if you are able to cheat people you trust. If you don't know what your opponent is going to do next, then he's the same as you, and you are basically staring into a mirror, outwitting yourself. Just kidding.

Theo (*prays*)   You made a big mistake, almighty Zeus, you forgot to make a god for aviation. The big airlines are in danger, you know – I mean, there are new dangers, not simply the usual problem of falling out of the sky. Now there are bombs and hijackings. People *kidnap* airplanes now. But, listen, here is the genius of Mr Onassis. He has supposedly made a deal with the Palestinians. There's a man in Paris named Hamsari, or Hamshari or something; he's the PLO's ambassador to France – well, unofficial ambassador, but he's high up and close to Arafat.

Walks over to **Costa**'s *blackboard and writes the name 'Hamshari' on it.*

Theo   At least this is the rumour. Mr Onassis has given him a huge pay-off – a lot of money – not to hijack our planes. I think that's brilliant. Well, it's just a rumour. It seems you also forgot to make a god for rumours.

Dimitra (*prays*)   Almighty Aphrodite, go away! Who needs a goddess of love? I used to think that love was simple. I was married for thirty years, and I won't claim it was easy, but it wasn't complicated – laundry, flowers, unspoken yearnings, shattered dreams – just what you'd expect. I never imagined the part that power and possession played. I mean – would Mr Onassis have loved Madame Callas if she hadn't had the most glorious voice in the world? Would he? It doesn't matter that he hates opera, that he says it always sounds like a bunch of Italian chefs screaming risotto recipes at each other. She possessed a commodity that he wanted to own, which doesn't mean he doesn't love her. Or didn't. But now there's a more valuable commodity for sale. And, believe me, that stiffens his penis. This isn't a world I understand. It's perfectly familiar to you, I know, but then you're a goddess. Good luck to you, I say. You're just not someone I want to speak to. You and what you represent are unknowable.

Costa (*to audience*)   I imagine Aphrodite has always understood the allure of a private plane. Not to mention that old standby, jewellery. And flowers. Aristo was a very attentive suitor for four and a half years.

Lights rise on **Jackie** *dressing for dinner, watched by* **Aristo**.

Aristo   It doesn't become me.

Jackie   What doesn't?

Aristo   Being a suitor.

Jackie   I would think not. If you want something you take it, don't you?

Aristo   Indeed.

Pause.

Your esteemed brother-in-law suggested I liked to *grab*!

Pause.

Jackie   I asked him.

Aristo   You what?

Jackie   Asked him.

Aristo   *Asked him?*

Jackie   For permission.

Aristo   You spoke about *us* to that termite, that discarded foreskin, that . . .

Jackie (*laughs*)   Stop it.

Pause.

He's the head of the family. That's a concept you understand. It's very Greek

Aristo   It's not Greek to fuck the head of your family.

Jackie   Oh! You know your mythology better than that.

Aristo   Does he have a tiny prick?

Jackie   He asked the same about you.

Aristo   I would think you gave him an impressive answer.

Jackie (*laughs*)   Do men ever grow up?

Aristo   And what did he say?

Jackie   When?

Aristo   When you asked permission.

Jackie   Oh, he said you can't marry that asshole.

Aristo What a mundane insult. Can't he do better than that?

Jackie And I said give me one good reason why not. And he said it would cost him five states. They are the most predictable family in the world. He says he needs a Jacqueline Kennedy by his side. How can he run for president standing next to a Jacqueline Onassis? It is, pragmatically, a very good point, although I did point out it would be Ethel by his side, not me, Ethel, the mother of his eighty-three children . . . He claimed the voters wouldn't notice her. But of course *I'll* notice her. When she's First Lady. Having dinner parties in *my* house. Does he have any idea how I'll feel? Of course not. He's never thought about it. None of the men in his family have any sensitivity to what a woman actually feels. Jack didn't have a clue, you know. He had no antenna for people and yet total understanding of 'the people'. Sometimes I'd lie awake at night and think, how can someone with such global sensitivity be such a shit? Bobby's a bit more complicated. He wants to be a decent person, but his genes won't let him. And yet as a leader of men, he's much more than decent. You figure it out.

Aristo Why do you continue to sleep with him then?

Jackie Because it turns you on.

Aristo *bites her finger.*

Jackie It does, doesn't it? You don't want to have me, you want to *steal* me.

Pause.

He and I helped each other get through it. Can you understand that?

Aristo Of course. Grief is famously erotic.

Jackie Don't be pretentious. Grief is hell – but you learn to accommodate it.

Aristo Does Bobby call me 'The Greek'?

Jackie Yes.

Aristo   I knew that cockroach-infested little midget would never call me by my name. Does he lick between your toes, like a cat, as I do? . . .

Jackie   Please! He's American, for God's sake.

Pause.

Sometimes I feel safe with him.

Pause.

Not *for* him, by the way; I think he's making himself a very easy target. But then I think that men like you and Bobby can excuse your behaviour, even *enjoy* your behaviour, if you know that some day you'll be punished. You are alike, you know. Well, not entirely. You don't share Bobby's distaste for social wrongs. You probably perpetrate them, my dear. You don't care – as he does – about the inequalities of society and the sufferings of the underprivileged. No, don't say anything. It's not your conscience that attracts me. So I asked him how profoundly it would fuck him up if I married you and he said, 'Profoundly.' Then I asked if we waited until after the election – would he then give us his blessing. And he said, reluctantly, yes.

Aristo   And you believed him?

Jackie   I don't know. He'll do anything to win an election. Even lie to me. And he does care about me. But you see, he thinks that America has lost something – something *moral* – at its core.

Aristo   Oh, and that two-bit politician, the third and lesser son of the bootlegger, cares about morality?

Jackie   Of course. Don't you understand that that's the contradiction that makes him so attractive? He wants to save his country. What is it you want to save? The problem is, he believes that if you really want to change society for the better, you have to be in a position to do so, and he thinks you can only arrive at that position through unethical routes. That's the way it is. So, yes, of course, he would lie to me.

Aristo   As, indeed, I would. (*Smiles.*) You're in what my Jewish friends call a pickle.

Jackie   Umm . . .

Pause.

I pass myself on magazine covers all the time. I never read the articles. It doesn't matter. I'm trapped, trapped inside other people's words – worse, I'm stuck in my *own* memoir, abandoned in my own life, unable to get the hell out. Can't someone tell me how to get out?

Aristo   You follow the string.

Jackie   And where does it lead?

Aristo   To the one who pulls it. (*Bites her ear.*) I have secrets that ambulance-chaser, that minute scrotum, your little brother-in-law, has never dreamed of. He's an amateur. Follow my string. It leads to freedom. And safety. Safety for you and your children. Safety, of course, is expensive. It's a much finer gift than a palace or a ruby, which I will also give to you. But they are replaceable; safety is not. (*Kisses her.*) Homer was wrong. The siren song was sung by a man.

Starts to make love to her.

The lights fade.

The **Chorus** *sing.*

Chorus   *Ksipna mikro mou ki akouse*
 Kapio minore tis avgis
 Gia senane eene grameno
 Apo to klama kapias psichis.

Costa (*to audience*)
 Wake up, my little one, and listen
 To a serenade of dawn
 Written especially for you
 Out of a weeping soul . . .

The song is interrupted by gunshots.

Gunshots again.

Dimitra   *Almost* as famous.

Yanni *runs into* **Aristo***'s office.*

Yanni   I've just heard the news.

Aristo   What news?

Yanni   On the television. Seriously speaking, it's bad news.

Aristo   What news?

Yanni   About Kennedy.

Aristo   What do you mean?

Yanni   Bear in mind, it's not surprising.

Aristo   *Yanni! Tell me the news!*

Yanni   Well, if I may be permitted to say so, someone shot him.

Aristo   Bobby?

Yanni   Yes.

Aristo   Is he dead?

Yanni   I think the specifics of his condition warrant –

Aristo   Yanni!

Yanni   Yes. He's dead.

Aristo   Who did it?

Yanni   They arrested a young man. A Palestinian.

Aristo   Ah. Palestinian.

Yanni   With a double name. Sirhan. Sirhan. It happened in a hotel. In Los Angeles. In a kitchen. Full stop.

Aristo   Someone was going to fix the little bastard sooner or later.

Aristo *goes to the* **Chorus***, who are singing the song he sang at the Kennedy wake.*

Chorus
> *Ke pou na rikso*
> *To megalo mou kaimo*
> *Opou na aniksi I gis*
> *Ke tha raisi to vouno*
> *Ilie fonia pos afises na gini to kako*
> *Skotosane to stavraeto*
> *Ke ton avgerino*
> *Kato sto stavropdromi*
> *Skotosane to nio.*

Costa (*translating, to audience, during song*)
> Who can I blame
> for the huge thorn in my flesh?
> It will open the earth
> And break the mountain.
> They killed the golden eagle,
> The morning star,
> Down in the crossroad,
> They killed the bright young man . . .

Chorus
> *Ke ta koritsia*
> *Riksan kato ta malia*
> *Gia na piastis aite*
> *Na anevis ap ti lismonia.*

Aristo   I sang that song to him in Washington. He disliked it. And now you sang it *for* him? He also disliked irony. He doesn't know what he missed. I must phone Jackie and offer my condolences. She's free of them now. The Kennedys. The last link just broke. I imagine this time I *won't* be invited to the funeral.

He walks away..

Dimitra (*to* **Costa**)   Your hero? In the classics, when an enemy dies, the heroes are humble.

Eleni   They pay tribute.

Theo   They show respect for a worthy adversary.

Costa   He may be many things, but he is *not* a hypocrite! I respect a man who doesn't shed false tears. So should you.

Dimitra   Poor Madame Callas.

Yanni   Why?

Dimitra   He can marry the other one now.

Alexandro *enters.*

Alexandro   He mustn't. He mustn't marry her.

Eleni   It's not your place to say.

Alexandro   She just wants his money.

Theo   He says that about *your* girlfriend.

Alexandro   I hear she's asked for twenty million dollars up front.

Dimitra   She could price herself out of the market.

Yanni   She'll get three million plus one million for each of her children, if I may say so thank heaven there are only two, and Ari will be responsible for her expenses as long as the marriage lasts. And after his death a hundred and fifty thousand dollars a year for life. That's his offer. End of paragraph.

Theo   They will compromise.

Costa   They both understand that the shame of the market is not in being sold, but undersold.

Yanni   Bear in mind, corporate mergers are always difficult.

Alexandro   If there's a wedding, I won't go to it.

Eleni   Why do you care so much what your father does?

Alexandro   I don't. I don't give a damn. I hate him.

Pause.

I worry about him. Even the Singer was better than this.

Alexandro *leaves.*

Dimitra   Poor Madame Callas!

Maria *enters.*

Maria Nonsense. I wish them the greatest luck. If Mr Onassis and Mrs Kennedy are to be married, I am certain they will be very happy.

Pause.

I do not feel betrayed.

Pause.

They have every right to make their own decisions and to follow their own paths.

Pause.

Let me hear my voice. (*To* **Dimitra**, *desperately.*) My voice!

Dimitra *signals and Callas singing 'Vissi d'arte' floods the stage.* **Maria** *listens and begins to weep.*

Maria What was it about? How could I have been in touch with the gods? What did it have to do with *me*? Where did it come from? Apollo, oh Apollo, why did you choose me? Did you just look down from the sky and say, 'Oh look, there's a fat Greek girl, let's give her a gift from heaven. All she wants to eat is chocolate and cake, but no, let her have ambrosia, in her throat, nectar from Olympus, let her have the voice of an angel, let her larynx be a lyre, a flute, a violin, let all of the ugliness of life dissolve when she opens her mouth, let her give pleasure to a despairing human race, like one of those creatures who distracted Odysseus from returning home, let her make a sound that might shipwreck sailors, a sound so beautiful and sometimes so ugly at the same time that it could not possibly be mortal.' O blessed Apollo, I didn't want it, don't you understand, I did not want it. But once you gave it to me, yes, I had to become a high priestess, I had to guard the flame. You charged me to never let the flame die. And I disobeyed you. I watched the flame flicker and slowly fade and I did nothing because I had found my own siren song and it was sung by a cruel man in dark glasses. You have punished me, Apollo, you have made my entire existence numb, you have injected my soul with novocaine, and all I yearn for is death. But you are a god, and surely you understand vengeance. Then give me my vengeance. Punish him! Do you hear me, Apollo? Punish him! My dearest Ari, my love, my life, my fire, my *man*, I curse you, I curse you and I curse everyone who touches you, and I call upon the gods to hear me. Hear me, Apollo, hear my curse! Once I could have sung it, I could have stood in an opera house and sung my curse, and it would have been the most beautiful curse in the world, and people would have cried and grabbed each other and carried memories of my curse for the rest of their wretched lives, but now I can only speak it, pathetically, brokenly, in a voice that will no longer give you pleasure, but nonetheless *hear it*!

Falls to her knees.

If you still call yourself a god, if you still have any power at all, if you still control man's fate, then listen to my plea and . . . destroy him!

Another recording of her voice floods the stage. She looks up as if from a trance.

I wish them nothing but happiness.

Starts to leave.

Theo   She *does* go on about her voice.

Yanni   Shh . . .

Dimitra (*to* **Maria**)   You are in such pain.

Maria   Of course not. I am perfectly all right.

Dimitra   But you are suffering.

Maria   Nonsense. I am at peace with myself.

Dimitra   Please, don't leave. Stay with us.

Maria   With you?

Dimitra (*puts her arms around* **Maria**)   We can comfort you.

Maria   Thank you. (*Moves away.*) But I can't.

Dimitra   Why not?

Maria   You're the *chorus*!

Maria *leaves.*

Eleni   No good can come of this relationship. Alexandro is right.

Costa   Perhaps Alexandro is blind. Perhaps . . .

Eleni   What?

Costa   He loves her.

Yanni   Loves . . . ?

Costa   Yes, I know, it's too strong a word. But perhaps there is some kind of a *feeling* . . .

Aristo *and* **Jackie** *in his garden.*

Aristo   My island is shaped like a scorpion. So it is called Skorpios. At first the island was covered only with olive trees. I've added all the trees of the Bible – almonds, bramble, pine, oleander, figs. I planted many of them myself. I like to work my land. My grandmother taught me all I know about things that grow. Did you know the fig is the first of the fruits to be mentioned in the Old Testament? It provides shade, you see; to sit beneath one's own fig tree was the Jewish ideal of peace and prosperity. Look at this – a pine cone. My grandmother said if you cut it lengthwise, the mark on its surface resembles the hand of Jesus. All the Turkish Greeks knew things like that; the exact parameters of Christ's hand, for instance. Exile thrives on mythology. Still – there are mysteries in nature, aren't there?

Jackie   I suppose.

Aristo   And now the island will be yours as well.

Jackie   Joint ownership of fig trees?

Aristo   A vested interest.

Pause.

What are you thinking?

Jackie   That life has so many unexpected turns. And twists. And curves.

Pause.

Fig trees.

Pause.

I shall like it here.

Lightning. Thunder. Rain.

Dimitra   It's an October rain, that kind that comes and goes in the autumn on the islands in the Ionian Sea.

Yanni   That's a good omen.

Dimitra *glares at him.*

Costa *and* **Theo** *place wreaths of white ribbons and lemon blossoms on* **Jackie**'s *and* **Aristo**'s *heads and cross over them three times.*

Eleni   She has a huge heart-shaped ruby on her left hand surrounded by diamonds.

Dimitra   And two rubies hanging from her earlobes, also set in diamonds.

Theo   She looks like a million dollars.

Yanni   One million five.

Aristo *and* **Jackie** *drink from a golden goblet of red wine.*

Costa   And so they married. I must confess to having a slightly superstitious nature. I placed charms beneath the mattress of the nuptial bed.

Dimitra *and* **Eleni** *start to sing.*

Dimitra *and* **Elena**
  Micros aravoniastika
  Koroido pou piastika.

The others join them.

Chorus
  Ke pira mia bebeka mariola gia gineka.

Aristo *walks in, a drink in hand, very drunk. He continues the song with them.*

Aristo *and* **Chorus**
Sto gamo manga na souna
Na vlepes ti iche gini
San na mouna ipodikos
Ke perimeno diki.

Dimitra   You join us on your wedding night?

Aristo   Of course. Am I not the son of the people?

Dimitra *raises an eyebrow to the audience.*

Aristo (*pouring a drink from a bottle, then handing the bottle to* **Costa**) Another drink? My wife is asleep. She's not a fan of carousing. Luckily, we had our honeymoon night several hours before the marriage ceremony.

Costa (*smiles*)   Shame on you.

Aristo   Well, didn't you notice that her Valentino dress was crumpled? The three left buttons were not properly fastened; they were in the wrong loopholes. She has the heart and mind of a classy cocotte. I always admired the girls at Madame Claude's, as you know. I admire my wife.

Costa   To see your bride before the ceremony on the day of the wedding is considered to be bad luck; to make love to her is tempting fate.

Aristo   Ah, fate. Ah yes. Fate.

Pause.

My wife has cost me a lot.

Costa   You did make a considerable settlement.

Aristo   I'm not talking about money. I'm talking about my *soul.*

Costa   Don't exaggerate.

Aristo   I'm not. My soul, Costa, my soul. Do you know who owns it?

Costa   Who?

Aristo   Hamshari. (*To the others.*) I thought we were singing.

Aristo *and* **Chorus**
Ke vgiki I apofasi
Pos ime pandremenos
Na kouvalao kathimernos
San gaidaros stromenos.

Costa (*in the middle of the song, to audience*)
I was like a man in custody,
Awaiting trial,
And then the verdict was announced –
I was married!

Aristo *and* **Chorus**
Erira ti gineka mou
Perno to bougiourdi mou
Ta sea mou tam ea mou
Ke pao gia to tsardi mou.

Aristo   Leave me, please.

He puts his hand on **Costa***'s shoulder, and motions for him and* **Yanni** *to stay, as* **Dimitra, Eleni, Theo** *and the* **Musicians** *leave.*

Aristo   Gentlemen, I believe I told you that I had paid Mahmoud Hamshari three hundred and fifty thousand US dollars as protection money. I wasn't quite telling you the truth. I have actually agreed to pay him one-point-two million dollars.

Yanni   One-point-two?

Aristo   One-point-two. (*Smiles.*) Million.

Yanni   But that's, I would like to say, an exorbitant amount of money. How much are the other airlines paying?

Aristo   That's beside the point.

Yanni   Don't you think we should find out?

Aristo   Nonsense. The other airlines won't admit that they're being blackmailed. Nor can we. We mustn't raise questions about Olympic's safety.

Yanni   But that, if I may call it a spade, is practically extortion.

Aristo   It *is* extortion, Yanni. That's the point. All right. That's all. You will have to do some creative accounting. It was on my mind. I wanted you to know. Goodnight.

Yanni *hesitates, then leaves.*

Costa   So. You *have* been keeping secrets.

Aristo   Sometimes I must. Even from you. Tonight this bothers me. But it will pass. I'm suddenly sober. I hate that. And I drank so much. Pity.

Costa   There's more.

Aristo   More what?

Costa   One-point-two million dollars, Aristo?

Aristo   This Mr Hamshari. He has an imperturbable face. That's a challenge. He does his homework, as well. As you know, I appreciate that. I suppose we have a lot in common. Exile and a desire for revenge. (*Pours another drink.*) Perhaps if I start again, sobriety will disappear.

Costa   And . . . ?

Aristo   And what?

Costa   What else do you want to tell me?

Aristo   Nothing. Goodnight.

Costa (*stares at him for a moment*)   Goodnight.

He turns to leave.

Aristo   What do you think of my wife?

Costa   She's a formidable woman.

Aristo   You preferred Maria.

Costa   I preferred Maria.

Aristo   I rescued my father and my family from the Turks, you know. My father was supremely ungrateful. I suppose he hated the fact that I had to be fucked by a man to do so. I decided to emigrate. I desperately wanted to come to America – oh America, everyone's dream then, wasn't it? – but they weren't welcoming too many immigrants from Turkey. So I bought a one-way ticket for a boat to Argentina. I was penniless. I had no idea what I was going to do with my life. I was totally adrift. That was forty-five years ago. And today I have married the most famous woman in the world.

Costa   And . . . ?

Aristo   And what?

Costa   Nothing. Goodnight.

Starts to leave.

Aristo   Hamshari handed me a slip of paper. He didn't want to say the name out loud.

Costa   What name?

Aristo   The designated name. Oh, do go to sleep. You're not following any of this.

Costa   You're talking in circles.

Aristo   I suppose I'm playing with you. Passes the time. Anyhow, I've always told you everything, haven't I? Sooner or later.

Pause.

I can't even call this a *drunken* confession. I'm so fucking alert. Well – he had told me about an idea of his. Evidently after the Six Day War he proposed to the Palestinian leadership that they assassinate a prominent American. A kind of wake-up call to America, to dissuade them from supporting Israel. A little crazy, isn't it?

Costa   A little.

Aristo   Well, it was too much for even Arafat; he thought Hamshari was a loose cannon and packed him off to Paris. Did you know any of this?

Costa   Obviously not.

Aristo   Hmm. You're slipping. I thought you had *sources*.
Anyhow, he still wanted to implement his idea and he asked
me to finance it.

Costa   Aristo! . . .

Aristo   You can't start being shocked by me now, my dear,
not after all these years. The liquor isn't working. He wrote the
name on a piece of paper. He *had* done his homework. He
knew how much I hated. I suspect Hamshari has an equal
capacity for hatred. I understand the man. He was expelled
from his homeland, just as my family was. Well, no matter.

Costa   And?

Aristo   Hence one-point-two million dollars. Far more than
the price of protection against hijackers.

Costa   I see.

Aristo   It wasn't just revenge. It was expediency as well.
Bobby would never have allowed me to marry her. He told her
to wait until after the elections, but he was simply stalling for
time. Hamshari said he could arrange for someone to carry it
off. I wasn't to be concerned about the particulars. And I must
say, he accomplished it with a certain degree of style. Of
course, from his point of view, the plan didn't really succeed;
the Palestinians were shocked and quite accurately denied any
responsibility, so they made no political gain whatsoever. I, on
the other hand, came out ahead. I was actually surprised it
happened. I thought I had thrown my money away. And I most
certainly don't regret it, that little cocksucker had it coming.
But it does take a rather prominent place in my thoughts, on
this evening, the evening of my marriage. I did, after all, pay
for the murder of the only man my wife ever really loved. The
odd thing is, it makes me desire her more. Yes, the liquor is
making me feel warm again. I had gone suddenly quite cold.

Pause.

Costa   Of course you don't know . . .

Aristo   Don't know?

Costa   If he really used the money to carry out that particular operation. He might have simply pocketed the money for himself. That event . . . that unfortunate event might have had nothing to do with you.

Aristo   Are you implying I was conned?

Costa (*smiles*)   I would never imply such a thing.

Pause.

Then tell me, why are you worried?

Aristo   Is that one of your wise little questions? I hate it when you pretend to know me. Go to sleep. I'm not worried. Not in the least.

Pause.

I would just be slightly more comfortable if it were a secret.

Costa   A secret?

Aristo   Well, if it hadn't been overheard – my conversation with Hamshari, that is.

Costa   But who could possibly have heard it?

Aristo   The gods, my friend, the gods.

Pause.

Sometimes they have a sense of humour about this kind of thing. Sometimes they don't. I think you should go to bed now.

Costa   Of course.

Pause.

Aristo . . .

Aristo   What?

Costa (*pauses*)   Goodnight.

Aristo *waves him off.* **Costa** *leaves.*

Aristo *starts to sing − the same song he sang on the boat.*

Aristo
>*Tha giriso lipimeni panagia*
>*Eche gia*
>*Min kles to marazi*
>*Mathe filakto na min kremas*
>*Na les den pirazi*
>*Tha'rthi aspri mera ke gia mas.*

Blackout.

Act Two

The **Chorus** *and the* **Musicians** *are onstage.*

Dimitra (*sings*)
 Argo to vima mes ti nichta
 Me tin varia vadizo
 Figane oliu ke m'afisan
 Na perimento kapio dilino . . .

Eleni (*to the audience, in the middle of the song*)
 I don't have a boat to travel on any more.
 There are no ports – or hearts – that will have me.
 Clouds cover the stars,
 It's a long wait for the dawn.

Costa *is at the blackboard. The names 'Niarchos', 'Eugenia', 'Tina' and 'Onassis' are written on it.*

Costa (*to the audience*)   A brief recap. Stavros Niarchos, married to Eugenia Livanos, sister of Tina, first wife of Aristotle. Niarchos divorces Eugenia, marries the heiress Charlotte Ford, love object of Stanislas Radziwell, husband of Lee, sister of Jacqueline, second wife of Aristotle. Niarchos divorces Charlotte and reconciles with Eugenia, whilst sleeping with Tina. OK? Got it? Well, things became difficult in the Niarchos household.

Giant puppets – one representing **Niarchos** (*voiced by* **Theo**)*, one* **Eugenia** (*voiced by* **Eleni**)*; one the* **Police Inspector** (*voiced by* **Yanni**)*.*

Or: **Theo**, **Eleni** *and* **Yanni** *might themselves be dressed as puppets, enacting the following scene.*

The **Eugenia Puppet** *screams, and falls to the ground.*

Niarchos Puppet   Oh dear!

Police Puppet   Dead!

Costa   Eugenia Niarchos was found dead on May 4th, 1970, on her bedroom floor, with an empty bottle of Seconal by her side. The autopsy report found multiple bruises on her body.

Police Puppet   A two-inch bruise on the abdomen with internal bleeding. Bleeding behind the diaphragm. A bruise on the left eye and swelling on the left temple. An elliptic haemorrhage on the right side of her neck. A haemorrhage to the left of her larynx with contusions above the collarbone on the left side of her neck, her left arm, ankle and shin. A ruptured spleen. How do you explain these injuries, Mr Niarchos?

Niarchos Puppet   Oh . . . Well . . .

Police Puppet   Well?

Niarchos Puppet   Well. Simple. Let me show you what happened.

The **Eugenia Puppet** *stands, drink in hand, looking into a hand mirror.*

Niarchos Puppet   I found her body on the floor. She had taken sleeping pills. I tried to revive her. I picked up her body –

Knocks the mirror and drink out of **Eugenia Puppet***'s hands.*

Niarchos Puppet   – and in doing so, I accidentally hit her abdomen –

Punches her abdomen; the **Eugenia Puppet** *screams.*

Niarchos Puppet   – and then, whilst trying to hold her upright, accidentally struck her diaphragm –

Whacks her diaphragm; the **Eugenia Puppet** *whimpers.*

Niarchos Puppet   – and, poor thing, she kept flopping over, and I kept trying to wake her up; I thought maybe a warm hand on her eye would wake her –

Hits her left eye.

– but I brushed against her temple.

Smacks her temple.

You see, my attempts at resuscitation were strenuous –

Hits her neck, her stomach, her arm, her leg; the **Eugenia Puppet** *is now unconscious and jerking to and fro and flying through the air, and the* **Niarchos Puppet** *is out of control, hitting, pulling and mangling the body, until he tears the puppet into little pieces.*

Niarchos Puppet   – but in the end I wasn't able to save her.

Police Puppet   Oh, I see. Yes, of course, Mr Niarchos, that makes sense.

Niarchos Puppet (*strangling the remains of the* **Eugenia Puppet**)   My poor wife . . .

Costa   Well, we will never really know what happened.

Aristo *enters, holding up an envelope.*

Aristo   Don't be so sure.

Dimitra *sings.*

Dimitra
  Mono gia menane karavi
  Den echi pia na taksidepso
  Ke ta limania ke I kabi
  Ke I kardies m'afisan ekso.

  Sinefa skepasan t'asteria
  Argi poli na ksimerosi
  O kosmos rimakse gia mena
  Kathos apelpismena perpato.

Eleni
  My world is in pieces
  And I am desperate.
  I don't have a boat to travel on any more
  And there are no ports – or hearts – that will have me.

Alexandro *walks through the* **Chorus**, *a Manila envelope in his hand.*

Alexandro   You're as bad as my father. You can turn everything into *rebetika*.

Costa   You don't believe in bouzouki nights?

Alexandro   Singing, dancing, drinking, breaking dishes, Melina, Zorba. No, I don't believe in it.

Alexandro *goes into* **Aristo***'s office.*

Aristo   I'm ordering more eucalyptus trees for the island. I like the way the perfume of the eucalyptus trees mingles with the smell of the salt.

Alexandro   What salt?

Aristo   From the sea, what do you think? You're so linear. You have no poetry. What the fuck do you want?

Alexandro   You're in a good mood today.

Aristo (*picks up some papers*)   Have you seen these? Bills! Dresses!

Alexandro   Are you wearing dresses now?

Aristo   Don't be a smart-arse. I married a walking credit card. Don't say anything. What are you doing here?

Alexandro   You have the goods on Stavro, don't you?

Aristo   What?

Alexandro   Uncle Stavro.

Aristo   I hate it when you call him that. You know, in ancient Greek, eucalyptus means well covered. An interesting term. Not necessarily applicable to your *Uncle* Stavro any more.

Alexandro   You have transcripts of phone conversations, don't you?

Aristo   Why don't you come and help me plant them? Work up a sweat for a change. You're becoming effete.

Alexandro   You have transcripts. You bugged his house and you have transcripts.

Aristo   You're repeating yourself. That woman of yours is making you senile. You need a charge account at Madame Claude's. The trouble with you is you've never paid for it. Yes,

I have transcripts. The eucalyptus, like most of my trees, is mentioned in the Bible, did you know that?

Alexandro   I don't care about trees!

Aristo   You should! You should love the earth!

Alexandro   Look – Stavro told the inquest that Aunt Eugenia was unhappy because she overheard a phone conversation he had with Charlotte Ford and so she swallowed a bottle of sleeping pills. But actually she overheard a conversation he had with Mother, isn't that true? Aunt Eugenia discovered that her sister – my mother – your wife – was his lover. And they got into a fight. And then who knows what happened. Well. Aunt Eugenia's dead. And you have all of Stavro's phone conversations of that evening on tape. Which, I assume, trashes his cover story.

Aristo   You have a one-track mind, which is fine, except the trick is never to show it.

Alexandro   What will you do with them?

Aristo   I haven't decided. I have so many delicious choices. What's important is that after all these years, *I have him*! How do you know all of this?

Alexandro   Mother. She took my sister to lunch. And she gave this to her. Here.

Hands him the envelope.

Aristo   What is it?

Alexandro   Open it.

Aristo   Don't you dare give me orders.

Alexandro   Oh, please. Just open it.

Aristo   From your mother?

Alexandro   Yes.

Aristo   It might explode.

Alexandro *stares at him.*

Aristo   All right, all right. Have it your way. Be serious.

He opens the envelope. He takes out some papers and glances at them.

Ah.

Pause.

I see.

Alexandro   Transcripts of conversations you've had with Costa. They have, of course, taped you too. And you know that poor patsy, the one who pulled the trigger, Sirhan Sirhan, left notebooks behind. There's a copy of some fragments from one of those notebooks here. The name Fiona is scrawled on one page. Fiona! Demented Mid-Eastern assassins don't usually speak the name Fiona, let alone write it in a notebook. And, on another page, there's the name Niarchos, spelled wrong, but still unmistakable. What did you do, make some kind of package deal? Were you going to have them killed as well? I mean, are you totally mad? Where do you live – in some kind of malevolent never-never land?

Aristo   Your mother gave these to you?

Alexandro   You may have him, but it seems that he has you as well.

Aristo   Your mother actually asked you to read these?

Alexandro   Doesn't matter. Those are copies. I've put the originals in a safe. If anything happens to Fiona – do you understand me? – if you ever dare harm her – I will expose you.

Aristo   How could she allow you to read this? You have to forget all about this.

Alexandro   Maybe you're not following me. I've put the originals in a safe-deposit box.

Aristo   You must wipe this from your mind. And never, ever mention it to anyone.

Alexandro   Who am I going to tell? 'Hi, did you know my father paid for the murder of Robert Kennedy? You know –

Daddy – the tree planter – lover of the earth.' How about your wife? Maybe I should tell her? Well, I will tell her if Fiona is hurt. You understand me?

Aristo   Your mother is a selfish bitch.

Alexandro   That's neither here nor there.

Aristo   I don't know how she could do this to you.

Alexandro   You're the one doing, not her. Fiona is the woman I love and you want to kill her.

Aristo   Doesn't your mother care about you?

Alexandro   This has nothing to do with Mother. Why are you fixating on her?

Aristo   *Because you mustn't know these things!* Because it's dangerous. Knowledge is dangerous. At least when you're swimming in this kind of sea. Too many people, too many factions, too many secrets. You must stay out of this. It's not your world.

Alexandro   No, it's not. Thank God for that. OK, I've warned you.

Aristo   No. *I've* warned *you*.

Alexandro   Right, then. We're even.

Pause.

What will you do with your tapes?

Aristo (*shrugs*)   Bury them, I suppose. Next to the eucalyptus. And await the next round.

Alexandro   I will never understand you.

He leaves, and walks to the **Chorus**.

Costa   You know what your father would say?

Alexandro   What?

Costa   Understanding is overrated.

Alexandro   He's grotesque. He sucks up all my energy. Whenever I'm with him, I can hear my heart pumping. I keep waiting for someone to ask, 'What's that terrible noise?' But no one else can hear it.

Eleni   Yes, you've always loved him.

Alexandro   He would have killed Fiona.

Eleni   And he's always loved you.

Alexandro   Will I ever be free of him?

Silence.

Dimitra   Some things are best not answered.

Alexandro   Fiona's building a house in Switzerland. When it's ready, I'll move in with her. I'll go to university. I'll get a degree. I'll get a job. I'll walk away. Just watch me.

Aristo *enters, drunk, holding a liquor bottle and a glass.*

Aristo   Are you still here?

Alexandro   I'm leaving.

He leaves..

Aristo   He always says 'I'm leaving'. Usually as he's arriving. Why aren't you singing? How about 'Caiqsis'?

Dimitra   If you'd like.

Sings.

> Gel, gel kaiksi
> Gia vas, gia vas
> Mes tis polis t'akrogiali.

Aristo, *who is getting drunk, and the* **Chorus**, *join her.*

Aristo *and* **Chorus**
> Mes ti sigalia
> Mes tou caremiou
> Ti lithi
> Gel, gel kaksis.

Jackie *enters. She carries a book.*

Jackie What are you singing?

Aristo What does it matter?

Jackie I'd like to know. It's beautiful.

Aristo (*mimics her voice*) It's beautiful.

Jackie Yanni, you're looking very chipper today.

Yanni Thank you. The song is about a boat.

Jackie A boat?

Costa Yes. A caique.

Jackie Oh. That's a beautiful shirt, by the way, Costa.

Eleni From Turkey.

Jackie The shirt?

Eleni No. The caique.

Jackie Oh. Sorry. I love the way you're always so direct, Eleni. It's an admirable quality.

Eleni Thank you, Mrs Onassis.

Jackie The children appreciated the apricot cake. They thought it delicious.

Eleni (*beams*) Thank you, Mrs Onassis.

Aristo This is making me ill.

Theo The song is also about the owner of the caique.

Jackie Oh. A shipowner!

Theo Well, no, it's just a caique.

Jackie Oh, small beans, then. But quite a different world than aviation, isn't it, Theo?

She flashes him her most radiant smile.

Theo Yes.

Jackie   But as interesting?

Theo   Well, in the song, yes.

Dimitra   It's the owner who is singing.

Jackie   And, Dimitra, did I thank you for the flower arrangements on the yacht last week? They were very tastefully done.

Dimitra   Were they?

Jackie   Oh yes. You have a 'touch'.

Dimitra (*blushes*)   I like flowers.

Jackie   And what is it that the owner is singing?

Dimitra
    Let's steal the beautiful woman,
    A slave in her own cell.
    She cries and grieves
    And asks for her freedom . . .

Jackie   Oh.

Dimitra   Do you like it?

Jackie (*smiles*)   'A slave in her own cell'?

Dimitra   Yes.

Jackie (*to **Aristo**, pointing to the liquor*)   May I have some?

Aristo (*pours her a glass*)   Don't drink *too* much. You're hardly a slave, you know.

Jackie   I never said I was. (*Drinks.*)

Aristo   Slaves don't spend thirty thousand dollars a month on clothing.

Jackie   That's overstated. Although I *am* high maintenance. You knew that.

Holds out her glass for another.

Aristo   Yes, well, paying for sex was always one of my weaknesses.

Jackie   An admirable one.

Aristo   The problem is sleeping with you is like fucking an ironing board.

Jackie (*a long pause*)   What would you know (*longer pause*) – about an ironing board?

Aristo (*amused*)   Almost as little as you, I admit.

Jackie   Anyhow, it's not true. You once told me I was like a diamond – 'cool and sharp at the edges, fiery and hot beneath the surface'. (*Laughs.*) Who's to argue?

Stands very close to him.

Do you like my perfume?

Aristo   I should. It probably cost twenty thousand.

Jackie   Ten. There was a sale.

Aristo   All that money on clothing and yet whenever I see you, you're wearing jeans.

Jackie   Well, my clothes are too nice to wear. That's a subtlety that has to do with market value; I thought you would appreciate it.

Aristo   I loathe subtlety.

Jackie   You're named after two masters of subtlety.

Aristo   What do you know about Aristotle or Socrates? You read an article about them? Don't talk to me about philosophers. *Greek* philosophers! Go away! I can't bear the sight of you.

Jackie (*laughs, holds out her glass*)   More, please.

Aristo   I thought marrying you would give me class.

Pours her another drink.

Jackie   There's no such thing. Not in our world, darling. It's like morality – it's a movable feast. You have it and you don't, both at the same time.

Aristo   The whole fucking planet is angry at me because I married you.

Jackie   I know, they think you're a promiscuous scoundrel. But you're my *second* promiscuous scoundrel. No one cared the first time. Maybe you should have married Maria.

Pause.

I know you're seeing Maria again. Do you know what upsets me?

Aristo   I don't care.

Jackie   It upsets me that you are photographed in public. The whole point of infidelity used to be that it was secret.

Pause.

I'll tell you what I would like more than anything. A quiet evening. Just the two of us, talking, or, nicer still, not talking. Reading. Sitting across from each other, reading, together. Think about it. (*To* **Chorus**.) Talk to him, my friends. Tell him he could have done much worse.

She leaves.

Dimitra   I hate to admit it, but she's right.

Costa   Why don't you have that quiet evening?

Aristo   Yes. In theory that would be nice.

Pause.

I can't.

Pause.

Anyhow, it's not my style. When have I ever had a *quiet* evening? She's trying to divert my attention. She knows I've been speaking to lawyers. About a divorce. It's tricky. Ever since I married her my most promising business deals have fallen apart. Beneath all the couturier clothing lies an evil eye. Of course, it might be different if she would deign to appear by my side at a business dinner. A Jacqueline Kennedy is a desirable consort when closing a deal. Well, I suppose it was a fantasy . . . And now just think of the kind of settlement she will demand. The problem is when you've been sleeping with a woman for several years, she has to be very stupid not to know at least one thing that could hang you. Even so, she has no real idea . . .

Takes **Costa** *aside.*

Aristo   Did you hear about Hamshari?

Costa   Of course. He was blown up –

Aristo   Answering his telephone.

Costa   By the Israelis. But evidently he didn't die. He's in hospital making a remarkable recovery.

Aristo   Not *that* remarkable. He developed a mysterious fever last night and now he's *really* dead. This time it was his own side that did him in. Supposedly. You can never tell, when it comes to that part of the world, who's killing who. As it is, Mossad and the Palestinian Secret Service are like Fred Astaire and Ginger Rogers. They make each other look good. Poor Hamshari knew too much. That's not a phrase I enjoy, my friend. *He knew too much.* I've dreamt about him, at least I think I have, I don't even remember what he looked like. My subconscious remembers. I can see him reaching for the fucking telephone. My nose for danger wasn't twitching enough, was it? What was I thinking? (*To* **Dimitra**.) You didn't translate all of the song, did you. There's a line about 'the oblivion of the harem'. Hah! 'Come, come caique owner . . . !'

Sings.

Gel, gel kaiksi
Na klepso tin giousel chanoum
Sklava mesa sto keli tis . . .

Theo, *who had walked offstage, returns with a wire in his hand.*

Theo   Mr Onassis, there's been an accident.

Aristo   Downhill, downhill, since I married her.

Theo   Your private jet crashed on the way to the island.

Aristo   Who was on board?

Theo   Just Dimitri and Giorgio, the pilots.

Dimitra   *Just?*

Aristo   And?

Theo   They're dead.

Aristo *registers this for a moment in silence, then turns to* **Costa**.

Aristo   It must have been sabotage.

Costa   Let's wait and find out.

Aristo   They're trying to kill me.

Costa   Who are 'they'?

Aristo   Does it matter?

Aristo *leaves.*

Costa   He's worried.

Yanni   He often worries.

Costa   No. This time he's frightened. That's different.

Alexandro *enters, agitated.*

Alexandro   Dimitri and Giorgio were my friends. No one knows what went wrong. Some people heard an explosion.

Eleni   The gods are unhappy.

Alexandro   I've been flying over the sea looking for wreckage.

Eleni   You should stay away from airplanes.

Alexandro (*brushes her nose*)   You're a silly old thing.

Dimitra   In olden days, if something fell from the sky it would have been a sign.

Aristo *enters and draws* **Alexandro** *to him and embraces him.*

Aristo   Life goes in cycles. I should never have married her. I might have overplayed my hand. I have enemies everywhere. When you have enemies, there's no such thing as an accident.

Alexandro   Wait a minute, you don't think this has something to do with Kennedy . . . ?

Aristo   Don't say it. It's not something we speak about. You know that. The walls have ears.

Alexandro   Look, this isn't *your* tragedy. This was an accident and I've lost two friends.

Aristo   I know, I know, it's difficult the first time you lose a friend. But it's part of growing up. You get used to it. You've never had to live through a war. You never had the Turks –

Alexandro   Please, don't tell me about Smyrna again.

Aristo   Listen, you brat, I'm trying to teach you something.

Alexandro   I've just heard those stories, over and over –

Aristo   A parent is supposed to repeat himself. That's what we do! Why can't you ever –

Alexandro   OK. I'm sorry.

Aristo   What?

Alexandro   I said I'm sorry.

Aristo   Oh.

Pause.

I am too.

Alexandro   You're what?

Aristo   What you said.

Alexandro   Which was?

Aristo   You know damn well.

Alexandro   What did I say?

Aristo   You said you were sorry and I said I was sorry. OK. Are you happy now?

Alexandro (*smiles*)   What are we sorry for?

Aristo   *It doesn't fucking matter!* Jesus! Go away. You get on my nerves.

Alexandro   OK, Pop.

He leaves.

Aristo (*shouts after him*)   Do not call me that!

Pause.

Wait!

Alexandro   What now?

Aristo   OK. All right. It's yours.

Alexandro   What's mine?

Aristo   The Puma.

Alexandro   Puma?

Aristo   The helicopter you asked me for.

Alexandro   Oh. I asked you last year.

Aristo   And I'm giving it this year.

Alexandro   Why?

Aristo   Who knows? I'm kind. That old amphibian, the Piaggio, it's ancient, you're right, we need a new one, it's a present, don't you dare thank me.

Alexandro   I wasn't going to.

Aristo   I'm not completely detached from human emotion, you know. I understand loss. And when you lose something, it's nice to have something else in return.

Alexandro   I don't believe this. I lost two *friends* . . .

Aristo   So you say.

Alexandro   You don't replace people with . . .

Aristo   What? *Things?* Oh, go away. You're just like Switzerland.

Alexandro   And you're like an endless novel, but I keep skipping a page –

Aristo   Homer, I hope.

Alexandro   He wrote poems.

Aristo   Actually, he was from –

Alexandro   *Don't.* Let's not start Smyrna again.

Aristo   You have your mother's eyes.

Alexandro   Is that good or bad?

Aristo   It just is.

*He kisses **Alexandro** on the lips.*

Aristo   It's not that you're stupid, I don't think that, it's rather that you're . . . dumb.

Alexandro   I don't want your gift.

Aristo   So don't take it.

*He stares at **Alexandro**.*

Alexandro *knows he has lost.*

Aristo *throws him the keys to the Puma.* **Alexandro** *grabs them and walks off.*

Aristo *goes to the* **Chorus**.

Aristo   What do you think? He's not so bad. He talks back. I never talked back to my father. I did make my way to Constantinople, however, with whatever I could salvage of the family fortune bandaged to my body. I spent weeks searching for my family; I thought they were dead. It was the first time I was ever alone. I recognised then that 'alone' was a condition of survival. And so I have remained ever since – does that surprise you? – despite the innumerable people who surround me and depend on me and even, in their pedestrian imaginations, 'love' me. Anyhow, I found out my old man was alive and bribed the right people – I discovered I had an instinct for that sort of thing – and sprang him from prison. He never thanked me. He said I had spent too much of *his* money on bribes. He said I was profligate. Really! In saving his life! That was my first lesson in futility. And so, at seventeen, I set sail for Argentina. My children are bored with these stories. It disturbs them that I was once a son.

Pause.

Shh! Do you hear it?

Costa What?

Aristo Quiet. Quiet's not healthy. I'm uneasy.

Costa What about?

Aristo Haven't a clue.

Pause.

I've never waited for anything in my life. And now I am. I'm waiting.

Looks up at sky.

They're waiting too.

Walks off.

Dimitra The sky is grey. A Greek sky should be blue.

Eleni Poseidon hasn't sent a wind from the sea.

Theo Apollo has hidden the sun with clouds.

Yanni But there is no rain. Zeus has forgotten about his thunderbolts.

Theo Wherever you look you can see – nothing special.

Costa He's right. The gods are waiting.

Dimitra Let them wait.

Eleni It seems pointless now to pray to them.

Yanni They won't listen to us anyway.

Theo Let's face it, they *never* listen. We keep praying to absentee landlords.

Dimitra Whatever will happen will happen.

Costa (*to the sky*) I suppose you think you're smart, up there on your Olympian heights. Actually, I've seen Olympus. It's not much. It's not exactly a Himalaya. You made a mistake, you know. You taught us about Fate, and once we embraced that concept, we started to despise you.

Dimitra Nothing is certain except for this – the gods will fuck you up.

Yanni *walks off.*

Dimitra *and* **Eleni** (*sing*)
    Sto pepromeno sou na dinis simasia
    Ken a prosechis pos vadizis sti zoi
    Otan kimase also grafi istoria
    Ke kapios pezi ti diki sou to zoi.

Costa (*to audience*) Basically, it means:
    You should pay attention to your destiny
    And the way you move in life.
    While you are asleep
    Someone else makes history
    And someone else plays with your soul.

Alexandro *encounters* **Jackie**.

Alexandro Oh.

Jackie Oh?

Alexandro Excuse me.

Jackie Yes?

Alexandro Father?

Jackie Office.

Alexandro   Oh.

Jackie   Oh?

Pause.

Alexandro   Tell him I'm taking the Piaggio out one more time.

Jackie   That's nice.

Alexandro   Then it's onto the scrapheap.

Jackie   The Piaggio?

Alexandro   Yes.

Pause.

Jackie   This has been the longest conversation we've ever had. Not to mention the deepest.

Alexandro   It doesn't matter any more.

Jackie   Why not?

Alexandro   You're heading for the scrapheap as well.

Jackie   Are you so certain?

Alexandro   Don't worry. He'll make a reasonable settlement.

Jackie   Do you think it's only the money I care about?

Alexandro   What else?

Jackie   Well – it's exciting, don't you think? The contradictions. The uncertainty. Treading on quicksand. Monsters attract me. Their mouths are dripping with blood because they've been devouring life – uncooked. They're a dying breed, you know. I meet the new ones now, the up-and-comers. The ones who are primed for power, the ones who will take over their organisations, their parties and ultimately their countries. They're faithful to their wives – honestly, can you imagine? – they're patriotic, they believe in God – one god, I might add, not the interesting variety that some of you still take seriously – and they are possibly even bearable parents. They may be rather similar to you. And yet, underneath, they're as empty and, I imagine, corrupt – and dangerous certainly – as the powerful always are. Perhaps more dangerous, because they always know they're right, unlike my first husband and his brother, who at least flirted with doubt; and they think too that they have values, unlike your father, who knows he possesses nothing of the kind. But he is peanut-butter chocolate laced with rum and strawberries. Whereas the future is vanilla. You should appreciate him while you can.

Pause.

Alexandro   I do.

Pause.

Jackie   Good.

Pause.

Alexandro   Tell him I was here.

Jackie   All right.

Pause.

You don't happen to know, do you . . . I mean . . . has he ever mentioned to you . . . the *size* of the settlement?

Alexandro *smiles and leaves. He walks through the* **Chorus***.*

Eleni   Where are you going?

Alexandro   One last flight.

Eleni   What?

Alexandro   On the Piaggio.

Eleni   No.

Alexandro   Tomorrow the Puma.

Eleni   You must never trust . . .

Alexandro   What?

Eleni   In tomorrow.

Alexandro (*kisses her forehead*)   Silly old thing.

Alexandro *leaves.*

Dimitra *and* **Eleni** (*sing*)
Oli echoume grameno
Pou to lene ppromno
Ke kannas dn mbori na t'apofigi.

Theo (*to audience, during song*)
We all have a future already written
It is called destiny
No one can escape it
There is no train or boat or even idea
That allows us to escape it . . .

Dimitra *and* **Eleni**
Den iparchi theoria
Oute trena oute plia
Ki o kathenas to palevi opos keseri ke mbori.

Theo
Ever since I was a child I dreamt of fire.

Chorus
Apo pedi ston ipno mou evlepa foties.

A hesitant **Yanni** *goes to* **Aristo**, *who is studying papers at his desk.*

Aristo   Yes, Yanni?

Silence.

He looks up, but clearly doesn't want to be distracted.

What is it?

Silence.

Say something.

Yanni   Let me put it this way, McCusker was going to
replace McGregor.

Aristo   Pardon?

Yanni   Well, to rephrase it, McGregor was going to show him how.

Aristo   Sorry?

Yanni   McCusker.

Aristo   Have you had a stroke?

Yanni   Your pilot. Donald McGregor.

Aristo   Yes. My pilot. I *know* he's my pilot.

Yanni   And he's leaving.

Aristo   Yes. I know he's leaving.

Yanni   And Donald McCusker is replacing him.

Aristo   So?

Yanni   So now it's clear what I'm saying.

Pause.

I think I'll leave.

Starts to go.

Aristo   Yanni!

Yanni   Yes, sir?

Turns back.

Aristo   What do you want to tell me?

Yanni   I don't *want* to tell you anything. But, bear in mind, they are both named Donald.

Aristo   *Who* are?

Yanni   McGregor and McCusker.

Aristo   I'm going mad.

Yanni   It's a coincidence, isn't it? Luck. Two Donalds. Perhaps it has some meaning . . .

Aristo   Yanni!

Yanni   Well – perhaps not.

Aristo (*puts his papers down and concentrates on* **Yanni**)   You are unequalled at figures, Yanni. That's why I keep you. Do you understand? It's the *only* reason I keep you. People think me intolerant. You prove that I am not. Still, you are an endlessly boring man. Now I want you to take a deep breath – obviously you are upset and you need to calm down a bit. All right? Breathe deeply . . . yes. Now try to construct a few simple sentences. And get to the point.

Yanni   Yes, sir. The point.

Aristo   The point.

Yanni   They went out with Alexandro.

Aristo   Oh? (*Suddenly nervous.*) Alexandro?

Yanni   Yes, sir.

Aristo   They?

Yanni   McGregor and McCusker, yes. Donald and Donald, as it were. Out. Full stop.

Aristo   Alexandro . . .

Yanni   On the Piaggia.

Aristo   Alexandro!

Yanni   McCusker had never flown one and McGregor wanted to show him.

Aristo   And Alexandro?

Yanni   Oh, he wanted, in a manner of speaking, to quote the boy himself, one last flight.

Aristo (*quietly*)   I think you better tell me.

Yanni   Yes, they said to tell you. But it's easy enough for them to say that . . .

Aristo   Please tell me.

Yanni   No, you see, unquestionably . . . there is a phrase, 'kill the messenger', and I do not relish this position, may I say −

Aristo   Listen to me very carefully. I want you to say what it is you are afraid to say. I will not hurt you.

Yanni   Do you promise?

Aristo   I promise.

Yanni   All right, may I just inform you −

Aristo   Quickly!

Yanni   There was, may I say, engine failure.

Aristo   *Engine* failure?

Yanni   The plane lost its balance, that's all. Like someone walking − very carefully − on a tightrope and then suddenly it, if I may use this word, dropped.

Aristo   Dropped?

Yanni   From the sky.

Aristo   (*softly*)   And my son?

Yanni   I think you should perhaps speak to the −

Aristo   *My son?*

Yanni   − hospital. Yes, they will notify you at the hospital.

Aristo   *Notify?*

Yanni   Well, present you with the particulars . . . the specifics, the . . .

*He cannot bear the look on **Aristo**'s face.*

The fact is, if I may put it this way, Alexandro's not . . . not still . . .

Aristo   He's dead.

Pause.

Yanni   Yes.

Pause.

Aristo   I see. Thank you, Yanni. You can go now.

Yanni *hesitates.*

Aristo   I've kept my promise. Go.

Yanni *starts to leave.*

Aristo *suddenly lunges at him and grabs his throat.*

Aristo   Liar!

He is strangling **Yanni***.*

Aristo   Fucking liar! Son of a whore! How dare you make up stories about my son!!

Costa *and* **Theo** *run in and pull* **Aristo** *off* **Yanni***.*

Costa   Aristo . . .

Aristo   My child. They have killed my child.

Costa   Aristo, Alexandro is amongst the angels now.

Aristo   What the hell good will that do him?

He waves the still-terrified **Yanni** *away and pulls himself together.*

Aristo   Someone will have to notify his sister. And his mother. And, I suppose, his woman.

He takes **Costa***'s hand.*

Aristo   You know, Costa, there are probably millions of people in the world at this very moment crossing themselves and saying, 'Thank God, I am not Onassis.'

Pause.

'Thank God I am not Onassis!'

He opens his mouth – an elongated, strangulated scream comes out.
Costa *leads him away.*

Eleni   Oh my golden boy. I brushed your hair, your beautiful long hair, every morning; electric sparks cracking in my hands,

my golden boy, just six, or was it seven? There was always –
what? – a thrill in it. How can I explain that? Perhaps there's
something not quite right about the way I felt. Perhaps a nanny,
by nature, is like a stew, a stew of misplaced feelings. But I did
love you, not quite as a mother, not quite as a woman, but love
nonetheless. My golden boy . . .

Sings.

> *Ilie fonia pos afises na gini to kako*
> *Skotosane to stavraeto*
> *Ke ton avgerino*
> *Kato sto stavrodromi*
> *Skotosane to nio.*

Theo (*to audience*)
They killed the golden eagle,
The morning star,
Down in the crossroad,
They killed the bright young man . . .

Costa (*returning*)   That song again . . .

Dimitra   No more. Sing it no more. 'The golden eagle, the
morning star.' What's wrong with us? Why do we always sing
about *special* people? Why do we mourn 'the bright young
man'? Not every young man shines brightly. Is the death of a
golden eagle more tragic than that of a pigeon? They both shit
on your head. What's the difference? My son died, you know.
Well, many years ago. My son died. He was seventeen. He was
a passenger as well. A car, not a private helicopter, a battered
two-seater, not a Porsche. He was not Hippolytus, a gorgeous
young man favoured by the gods, let alone an Alexandro. He
had spots. Lots of them. Covering his face. And his back. He
was having a horrible puberty. And his teeth protruded. And
he was overweight. His body had not yet discovered its shape.
He was not a golden youth. But he was my son. He had a
sweetness; if you looked you could find it. And he was funny,
in the way the unattractive often are. His death made no
headlines. But my heart – my heart – turned to ash, as if a
volcano had destroyed a once beautiful island, and now there

is only black sand to walk on, where once there was a holiday beach. Is my son's death less tragic than Alexandro's because I clean a boat that his father owns? Will someone write about my son's life and make him into a film? What is there to say about him – who knows what kind of man he would have been? But do you think Fortune is less cruel in its treatment of me than the great Aristotle Onassis? Or is it that life itself is very fair – finally it screws *everyone*.

Costa   But you, my dear, did not, I presume, offend the gods. There was no reason to take your son. Aristo, on the other hand, did unspeakable things. Do the gods not strike down the great when they are immoral?

Eleni   No.

Dimitra   Are you kidding?

Theo   They usually let them get away with it.

Yanni   But bear in mind, this was an accident.

Eleni   And yet we all knew it was his destiny, didn't we? Don't say we didn't.

Yanni   We have to be careful, in my opinion. If we can't blame the gods, where does that leave us?

Costa (*to audience*)   Well, as it happens, Aristo doesn't blame the gods. He blames everyone else.

Aristo *enters, holding an envelope. He is dishevelled and looks at least slightly deranged. He has been drinking.*

Aristo (*to* **Chorus**)   Well, what do you think? Tell me. Do you really believe it was an accident? Do you?

Dimitra   I'm afraid accidents happen, Mr Onassis. They are beyond our control.

Aristo   Oh really? Who asked you? No, there are too many questions. Too many unsolved mysteries. Why did a plane fall out of the sky on a perfect winter afternoon? I have a report from the air force –

Holds out envelope.

Here – read it. Reversed cables. That's what they found. The cables in the plane were each on the wrong side. Well, come on, read it.

Thrusts papers at them.

Who reversed them? Who wanted to kill my Alexandro? Who hated my Alexandro?

Theo   I don't think anyone hated him. He was a fine young man.

Aristo   Yes, he was.

Theo   Everyone loved him.

Aristo   Yes. Thank you, my friend.

Takes a big wad of cash out of his pocket.

Everyone loved him. Here.

Shows the money to **Theo***.*

Aristo   Buy yourself something.

He tries to give **Theo** *the cash.* **Theo** *resists.*

Costa   Aristo!

Aristo   No, no, take it.

Thrusts the money into **Theo***'s hand.*

Aristo   It's only money. What does money matter? Everyone loved my boy.

Theo   Yes. He was kind.

Tries to return the money.

Aristo (*refusing the money*)   No, take it, you idiot, take it. But did everyone love *me*? Ah, that's the question. What do you think?

Theo   Everyone respects you, Mr Onassis.

Aristo   Oh, for Christ's sake, give me back the money.

Grabs the cash back from **Theo***'s hand.*

Aristo   Everyone hates me – you know that. They – in particular – *they* hate me.

Yanni   Who?

Aristo   They. Them. *Others.* Here, I don't want it.

Hands the money to **Yanni***.*

Aristo   They killed my Alexandro to get to me. Don't you understand? It was an assassination by *proxy.* (*To* **Eleni***.*) You loved him too, didn't you? From the time he was a child. He was an attractive baby, wasn't he? I mean, taking into account that babies are always ugly, he was a looker, nonetheless.

Tugs the money from **Yanni***'s hand.*

Aristo   Give it to her.

Takes the money and gives it to **Eleni***.*

Aristo   Here. I want you to have this.

Eleni   No, Mr Onassis.

Aristo   Take it! I named him after my uncle, did you know that? He was a passionate man, very political. The Turks hung him in a public square. Turks! They are everywhere, disguised, waiting . . . Don't you believe me? Costa, the board.

Costa *wheels out the blackboard.*

Aristo (*to audience*)   Pay attention! (*To* **Costa***.*) Write these down. These are the possibilities. *Palestinians.* Well, that's obvious, isn't it? (*To audience.*) Isn't it?

Costa *writes 'Palestinians' on blackboard.*

Aristo   They were sending me a warning in code. My son's body was the code. Never, never speak about Hamshari. That's what they were telling me.

Costa   Aristo . . .

Aristo   If the world knew about Hamshari, they, the
Palestinians, would be totally compromised. They preferred
not to kill me, I might come in handy some day – some more
protection money maybe. So let's see, let's kill the son, that will
be our message to him. Kill the son. And Alexandro, of course,
stupid boy, knew what had happened, thanks to his mother, his
foolish mother, who told a child, a *child* – an innocent – things
he must never hear. And they knew he knew. There are more
listening devices in each of our houses than there are ice cubes.
And that made him even more disposable.

Costa   Aristo, you are saying too much. Let's go back to the
house.

Aristo   Excuse me? I give the orders, not you. Write. *Israelis.*

Costa *writes 'Israelis' on blackboard.*

Aristo   Another warning to me. If it were ever discovered
that Bobby Kennedy's death was directly tied to the upper
echelons of Palestinian leadership, well, yes, Israel would win
a few brownie points, but they would lose some as well – the
American people might get fed up with the entire mess and
wash their hands of it. They would, of course, assume I'd
blame Alexandro's death on the Palestinians. Just as the
Palestinians would assume I'd blame the Israelis. *Or* it could
have been Mossad and the Palestinian Secret Service working
in tandem. They have carried out joint operations, didn't you
know that? Don't muck around with the Middle East. That's
their message. And, of course, they're right. How could I have
been stupid enough to walk into that cauldron? Has that
disputed piece of geography ever led to anything but disaster?
Connect them, please. Draw some lines. Right.

Costa *draws lines connecting the Palestinians to the Israelis.*

Aristo   Then there's the CIA. The FBI. The Mafia.

Costa *writes 'CIA', 'FBI', 'Mafia' on the board.*

Aristo   Their message? How dare you kill a Kennedy! That's
what *we* do. Connect them.

Costa *draws lines connecting them.*

Aristo   And connect them to Israel and Palestine as well.

Costa *draws more connecting lines.*

Aristo   See how they criss-cross? They do each other's dirty work when it suits them. These days a bullet has many fathers. As do reversed cables. Connect them all! And throw in the oil companies – think how they must hate me, the ugly little Greek peddler, sailing his tankers into their rarefied Protestant domain. And don't forget Greece itself.

Costa *writes 'Oil' and 'Greece' on the board and draws connecting lines.*

Aristo   The colonels are frightened of me. The colonels are in bed with the oil barons and the oil barons with the CIA. Everyone's connected. Draw lines between all of them. They are all of them – Israel, Palestine, CIA, FBI, Mafia, oil and, yes, even Greece – all of them – Turks!

Pushes the blackboard away.

OK, the chart is finished. The gods have had their little joke, haven't they? Perhaps they had their own plans for Bobby and I screwed them up. Perhaps they were planning their own assassination along more classical lines. Perhaps they were grooming Ethel to finally throw in the towel and shoot the bastard herself. Or perhaps they really wanted him to be elected president – and what? – bring justice to the land? Well, perhaps he would have made the world a better place – fancy that. Odder things have happened. Whichever, I interfered with natural order, didn't I? It comes down finally to that, doesn't it? To me. The finger points directly to me. If I had simply given Hamshari protection money, nothing more, this would not have happened. My Alexandro would still be alive. My son would still be here – *annoying me* – annoying the hell out of me, the dumb prick, but *here* . . . (*Weeps.*) My son.

Eleni   No, no, it's not your fault . . .

Dimitra   You're just grieving . . .

Yanni   You're in shock . . .

Eleni   Don't blame yourself.

Aristo   Don't you dare give me sympathy. I do not accept condolences. I do not want pity.

Grabs the money from **Eleni**'s *hand.*

Aristo   Give it back. That's mine.

He leaves.

Theo   He looks terrible.

Eleni   He's making himself ill.

Yanni   He's consumed by grief.

Dimitra   He's drinking too much.

Theo   Do you really think Alexandro was murdered?

Dimitra   It doesn't matter. *He* thinks so. That's all that counts.

Costa (*to audience*)   He's been in and out of hospitals. His body is breaking down. He has a disorder of the autoimmune system. It usually hits men in their forties. He's proud of that, says it shows what great shape he's in. I think he's dying.

Jackie *enters.*

Jackie   Oh dear.

Costa   What is it?

Jackie   I missed him in the hospital. He's back on the island now.

Costa   Oh.

Jackie   Well . . .

Pause.

Costa, I know.

Costa (*frightened*)   What do you mean?

Jackie   I know what he did.

Costa   You do?

Jackie   It's hard to forgive him.

Costa   Yes, it must . . . how did you discover . . . ?

Jackie   I overheard a telephone conversation. He's become careless. How could he do it?

Costa   I don't know. I'm . . . I'm so sorry . . .

Jackie   I mean . . . drugs, of all things.

Costa   *Drugs?*

Jackie   Yes. The Caribbean venture. I know all about it.

Costa *starts to laugh.*

Costa   Drugs.

Jackie   Why is it funny?

Costa   It's not. I'm sorry. Nerves.

Jackie   He's running drugs. It's so undignified. His tankers are transporting heroin from the Caribbean. Do you know how many young people that kills? How can you be a part of this, Costa?

Silence.

Has this been going on for a long time?

Costa   It's recent. Since he's been ill.

Jackie   Why? Doesn't he have enough money?

Costa   Cashflow problems. He needed cash.

Jackie   What for?

Costa   A divorce.

Jackie   Oh.

Pause.

Costa How can I be a part of this? If you are attached to his life, you can afford a lot of soap.

Jackie I thought he was a pirate, not a gangster.

Costa Can you be one and not the other?

Jackie Probably not.

She starts to leave, then turns and speaks, almost to herself.

Tick-tock . . . tick-tock . . .

Costa What?

Jackie Nothing.

She leaves.

Yanni *rushes in.*

Yanni She's dead.

Costa Who?

Yanni His wife.

Costa What?

Yanni His wife, permit me to say it, has died.

Costa His wife?

Yanni Mr Onassis' wife.

Costa Are you insane?

Yanni Bear in mind, they've been divorced many years.

Costa Oh.

Pause.

What happened?

Yanni I don't know. I was just told. Tina was found dead in Paris in the Niarchos apartment. Some say a heart attack, some say an overdose. Seriously speaking, according to the news reports, it took Niarchos twenty-four hours to report her death and the first person he phoned was not her doctor but his lawyer.

Dimitra   Misfortune is a party animal, it loves a crowd.

Eleni   The mother of his children.

Yanni   How much more can he take?

Theo   At least he can't blame himself for this.

Eleni   Where is he now?

Costa   On the island, where he always is, at Alexandro's grave.

Aristo, *very frail, a blanket over his shoulders, sits on his haunches, in front of a grave.*

Aristo   Now, your mother. Fourteen when I met her. I wasn't usually interested in 'green fruit' as we called it then. But she had golden hair and a tantalising smile and she already knew how to lie. And her father was the wealthiest shipowner in the world. Do you smell the eucalyptus? You don't care about trees, do you? Well, tough shit, you're surrounded by them. And it's just as I told you – the eucalyptus blends with the salt from the sea. It's an extraordinary smell. Yes, she was a valuable prize, your mother. As was my second wife. Sometimes I hear melodies. Old popular Turkish tunes. In my head. There were musicians – just a few – that played in a cafe in Smyrna near the harbour. Smyrna was the ancient home of demigods, did you know that? Mandolins, zithers, guitars. There were almond trees – trees again, sorry, can't help it – jasmine, mimosa. No, my second wife was an even more valuable prize. There was nothing like her on the market. And at the time the price didn't seem like that much, really.

His voice gives out; it's difficult for him to speak.

Forgive me. (*Whispers.*) Forgive me.

He pulls himself together and gathers a bit of strength.

The whores at Madame Fahria's were exquisite. They smelled of body powder. Coloured silk stockings. Fancy underwear. I was only fifteen, but I was learning. The fact that you had to pay for them only made them more desirable. You see, I fell in love – I fell *in love* – with women and transactions at the same time.

Pause.

I think eventually you'll grow to like eucalyptus.

He tightens the blanket around his shoulders.

The **Chorus** *have been watching in dismay.*

Eleni   Surely someone must cheat Fate sometime.

Dimitra   I think if you do, the point is to keep it a secret.

Theo   Anyhow, we misidentify who we pray to. It's really just a tax collector up in the sky. Sooner or later, we have to pay.

Costa   And when it's over – when his light is extinguished – what will happen to me?

Theo   You can bathe in it, friend, for a long time after. There will be foundations to look after. And memoirs. I wouldn't worry.

Yanni   Bear in mind, some charities will benefit.

Dimitra   In time he'll become what you always wanted him to be – a hero.

Eleni (*to the* **Musicians**)   I think you should play. (*To the others.*) At the end of the day, there is music.

The **Musicians** *start to play 'Aspri mera kai gia mas' – the song from the boat.*

Costa (*to audience*)   He goes to the hospital one last time. The doctors can do nothing. He is just fading away. Jackie visits sometimes, Christina often. Otherwise, it's impossible to get past the guards.

Maria *sits on a chair, next to a hospital bed. The bed is covered by a screen.*

Maria   At the end of the day there is music. Did you hear that, Aristo? Music. I think it soothes the savage – what? Shall I sing for you, my dearest? Would you like that? One last serenade.

Maria *sings. Her voice is practically non-existent.*

Maria
> *O mio babbino caro*
> *Mi pica e bello, bello*
> *Vo'andare in Porta Rossa*
> *A comperar l'anello*
> *Si, si, ci voglio andare*
> *E se l'amassi indarno*
> *Andrei sul pont Vecchio*
> *Ma per buttarmi in Arno*
> *Mi struggo e mi tormento*
> *O Dio, vorrei morir!*

Pause.

And that, my dear, is the last time Maria Callas will ever sing. And she sang it for you, my love. For you. To show you what you destroyed. I mean, tell the truth, wasn't it awful? There is no voice there. Once there was – such a voice. But when it's gone, it's gone, as spectacularly as it once was present. It does irritate me that you are filled with remorse at destroying a distant politician when you don't have an iota of regret about my voice. I wonder which history will view as the greater loss. Oh dear! Listen to my vanity.

She pulls the screen away. **Aristo** *lies still – attached to tubes, his eyes closed.*

Maria   Look at you – a spaceman! Isn't it ironic that after years of not listening to me, Apollo finally answered a prayer, and this is the result. I guess he only takes you seriously when you ask for bad things to happen to other people.

She throws the screen down.

Paw, paw, paw. This isn't you, Aristo. You were never connected to anything or anyone, let alone a tube. Let's get rid of them. Nasty things.

She pulls the tubes out of his body and pushes his body up in the bed into a sitting position.

I know you couldn't care less about Puccini, my darling, even had it been well sung. You want your own kind of music, don't you? Taverna music. *Rebetiko.*

Aristo *opens his eyes.*

Maria   Come with me, then.

She gives him her hand. He rises from the bed.

She leads him to the **Chorus** *and* **Musicians**.

The **Chorus** *are once again distributing sweets to each other and pouring glasses of wine.*

Suddenly **Aristo** *hesitates and is afraid.*

Maria   No, you don't have to wait. There's nothing to wait for. It's all right. I'm dead. We're all dead. We're all memories now. Ash. Dust. Whatever. And soon a wind will come from the east – from Smyrna perhaps – and blow even that away.

Chorus (*sing*)
  Tha giriso lipimeni panagia
  Eche gia
  Min kles to marazi
  Mathe filakto na min kremas
  Na les den pirazi
  That'rthi aspri mera ke gia mas . . .

Maria (*interrupting, to* **Musicians**)   Please – play a *zeimbekiko*. I want Aristo to dance.

The **Musicians** *play a* zeimbekiko.

Maria   The way he would dance for hours in the taverna, ignoring me, humiliating me. The way he would dance when he cheated on his mistress and his wife and his lovers as well and even the ladylike whores from Madame Claude's who were waiting in the wings. The way he would dance when he had finessed a business deal that was so intricate and — well, Byzantine — that only a genius — or a Greek — or, actually, a Turkish Greek — could ever understand it. The way he would dance when he was hungry — hungry for food, for wine, for love, for intrigue, for power, for sex, for pain, for deceit . . . The way he would dance when he was alive.

She lets go of his hand.

Damn you, Aristo. Damn you, my love. Dance.

Aristo *dances as:*

Curtain.